Half Guard and other BJJ Fundamentals

by

Marcelo Giudici

&

Andrew 'A.J.' Morales

MARCELO GIUDICI

Half Guard and other BJJ Fundamentals

Coauthored by A.J. Morales

This book is dedicated to Ryan Gracie whose memory will live on in those who loved him.

Table of Contents

Table of Contents

Drills for Passing Opponent's Guard
- Guard Pass Drill 1
- Guard Pass Drill 1 - Application
- Guard Pass Drill 2
- Guard Pass Drill 3
- Guard Pass Drill 4
- Guard Pass Drill 4 - Application
- Guard Pass Drill 5
- Guard Pass Drill 5 - Application
- Guard Pass Drill 6
- Guard Pass Drill 6 - Application
- Guard Pass Drill 7
- Guard Pass Drill 8
- Guard Pass Drill 8 - Application

Appendices
About the Coauthor
Acknowledgements
Marcelo Giudici Martial Arts Career

Purpose of this Book

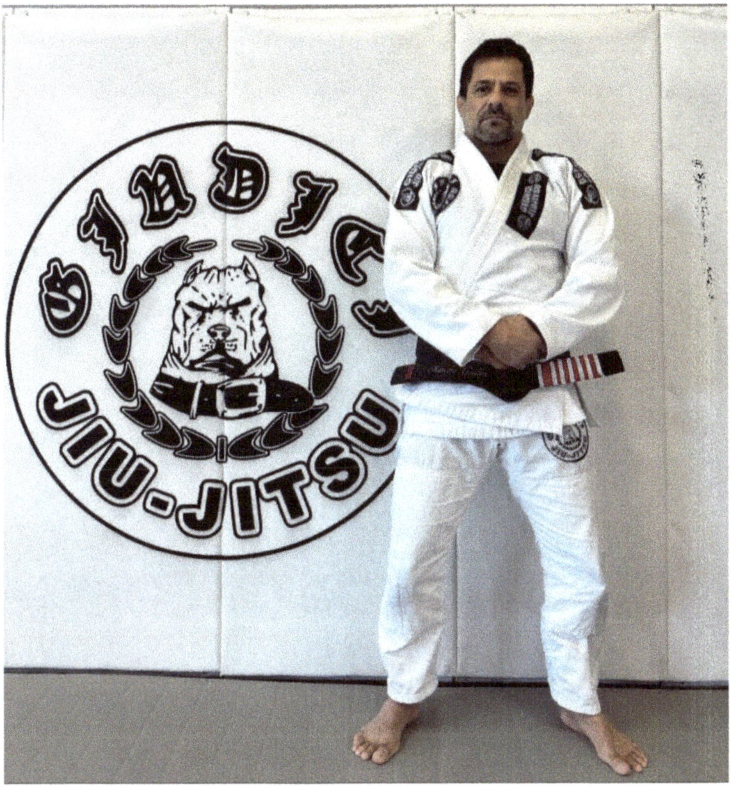

MARCELO GIUDICI

5x São Paulo Sate Champion

Bronze Pan American Champion

Bronze Mundial Rio De Janeiro Champion

Real Vale Tudo champion, 14-win, 2-loss record

WRITING THE BOOK

This will be my first book which I have wanted to write for many years but haven't had the opportunity. I have published videos for teaching techniques in other countries but writing a book is so much more. You can put your life into a book.

Now that I am in the United States, I felt that this was the best time to start writing books about my favorite techniques that I have learned and honed over the years of fighting and competing in BJJ. This book will focus on the half guard and include basic, intermediate, and advanced techniques that are easy to do and are very effective.

The book will have detailed techniques and drills that will grow your abilities which will be good for white and black belts. The success of this book will help me continue to publish more books in the future.

The book doesn't only include the techniques but also includes my philosophy that people can read more about. I became very effective in passing guard, and half guard, because I studied and trained each of these positions so much that I am confident that these techniques will work for you.

- Marcelo Giudici

How to Read

TECHNIQUE OVERVIEW

Each variation in the book will start with a complete step-by-step list of details that covers every aspect of the technique.

These steps will follow the tutorial provided in the subsequent pages and will include detailed pictures highlighting the major movements. At the bottom of every page are QR codes which you can scan with your phone's camera and will take you to the online video where you can become a member of our Patreon where we demonstrate the technique along with other training.

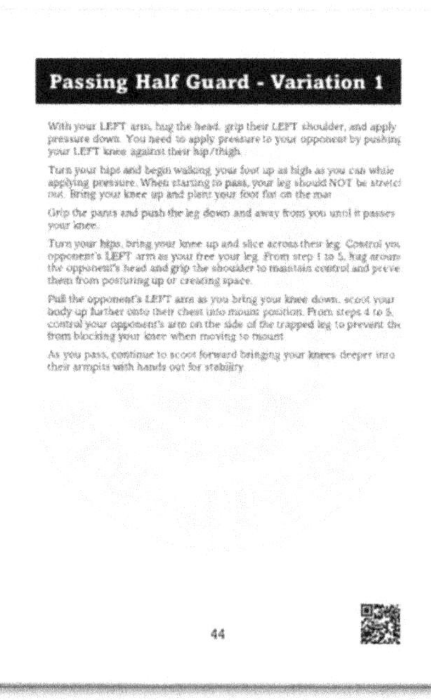

DETAILED STEPS

Each page will include a section dedicated to a single variation with step-by-step instructions with additional details that highlight important techniques.

These sections are read left-to-right following the numbered steps across the bottom of each page. The additional details are noted with alphanumeric characters that correspond with the steps across the bottom of each page.

In some cases, there may be alternative techniques provided that can be studied for added effectiveness of the technique.

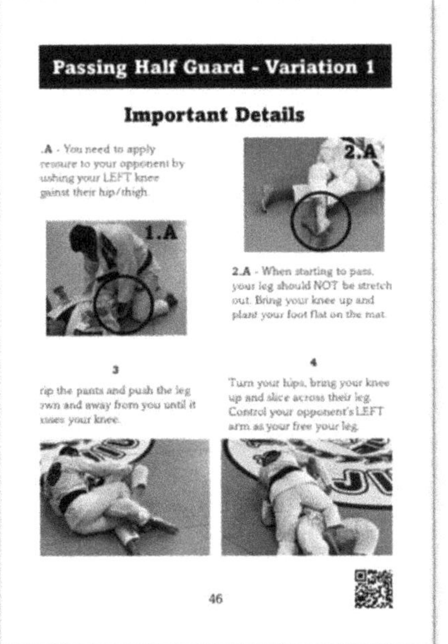

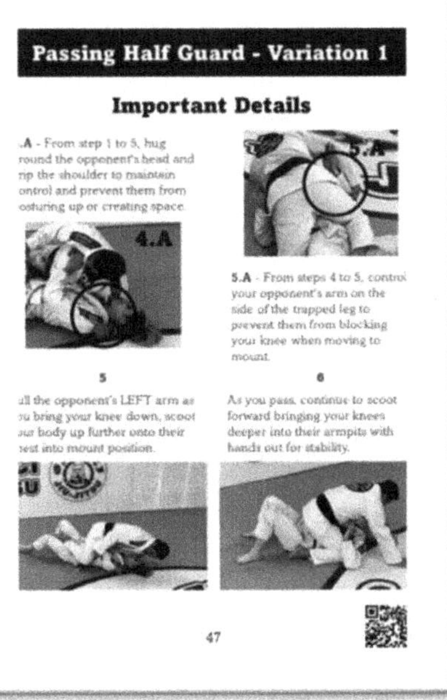

13

Master Joe Moreira is an 8th degree Brazilian Jiu-Jitsu Coral belt, 4th Degree Judo Black Belt, and an Original Ruas Vale Tudo Black Belt.

Joe fought in multiple UFC events, is a Judo Olympic trialist, and teaches seminars for his affiliates around the world, focusing on the fundamental principles of Brazilian Jiu-Jitsu that he has perfected over his 55 years of expreience in martial arts.

I've known Marcelo Giudici for around 40 years, and I have always loved the way he fights because of how he's always moving forward. We became good friends around 30 years ago when he came to train with me at my school.

When Marcelo came to California, we trained together for the first time. I found Marcelo to be very humble, very tough, and always gave lots of respect for the people at my school.

I became friends with him because of his vision for fighting, the way he supports people, his loyalty to people, and how dedicated he is to his students. I only have good things to say about Marcelo.

Marcelo had an open mind and didn't need to prove himself when we trained together. He understood that he isn't a big guy and he needed to build upon his techniques to make up for his size.

Marcelo learned a better way to fight that was more technical, with less power, and is much different than how Jiu-Jitsu is taught today. He adapted himself to "perfect" his game, his unique style of fighting, and his knowledge of passing the half guard.

When I was younger, I remember that I loved to fight and train Jiu-Jitsu from the bottom. Then I improved my top position and became more comfortable fighting in all positions as I got older.

My vision of Jiu-Jitsu has changed from 40 years ago because I do not have the power I used to have when I was 20 years old. Now, no matter what position I'm in, I'm comfortable because I understand my limitations.

My view of Jiu-Jitsu has changed and that is how I see Marcelo. He understands the better way he can fight and that is why he

Joe Moreira

knows half guard so well. He knew his limitations and has perfected his game.

Marcelo Giudici is a good instructor, he is dedicated to his students, and is a complete martial artist. He knows how to fight standing up, on the ground, MMA, and other sports. I believe that the United States will benefit from having Marcelo and the people of Northern California are fortunate to be able to train with him.

I hope more people come to check out Marcelo's gym and I know you will be happy with him. Marcelo loves to teach and is dedicated to his students. He knows when he needs to be tough on his students because this will improve their mental toughness. Marcelo will help prepare you for what's outside the mat.

- Joe Moreira

Professor Marcelo Giudici, Master Joe Moreira

Joe Moreira loves martial arts; his fighting career started in Judo where he is a 4th degree blackbelt and competed for the Brazilian team. He is an 8th degree Brazilian Jiu-Jitsu Coral belt, and an Original Ruas Vale Tudo Black Belt.

Joe is a Pan American champion, Judo Olympic trialist, and UFC veteran. Joe also competed in UFC 8 and 14 when there was no gloves and no weight division.

Joe is 60 years old, father of four children, and has one grandson. He teaches in seminars around the world, is the President and founder of the United States Federation of Brazilian Jiu-Jitsu and started the first international Brazilian Jiu-Jitsu tournament.

"I have had a lot of fights, but I would not call them mixed martial arts. Before MMA we would fight for honor, we would fight to defend our flag, and we fought to represent our schools."

- Joe Moreira

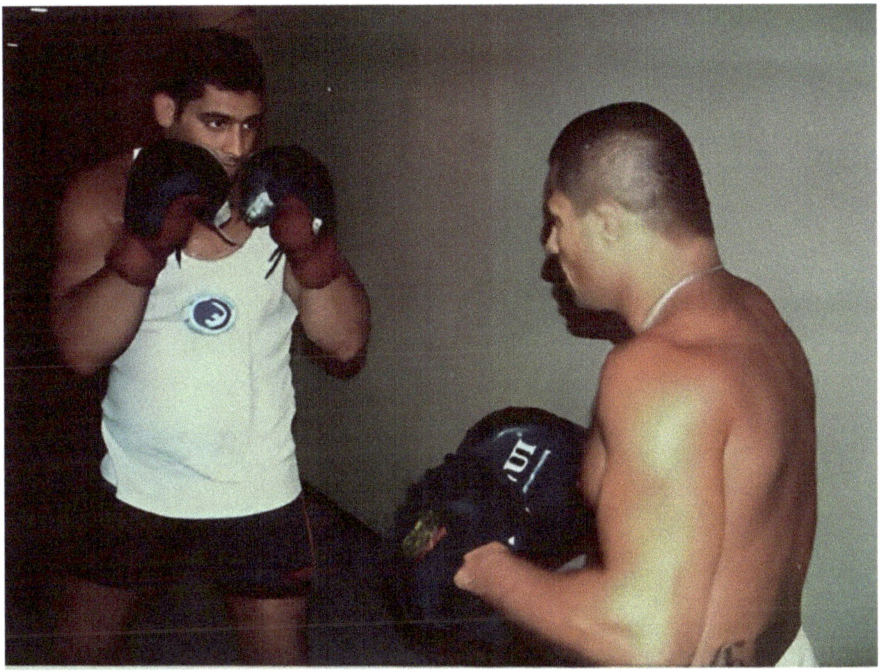

Professor Daniel Gracie is a 6th degree Brazilian Jiu-Jitsu black belt, a two-time World Champion in Brazilian Jiu-Jitsu, PRIDE veteran, and international Mixed Martial Arts fighter.

GRACIE KORE
柔術

Forward by Daniel Gracie

I have known Giudici for over 25 years, and I remember him being a monster in the bare-knuckle fighting.

When I first saw Giudici, he was fighting against Jiu-Jitsu guys when he was a kung fu and Chinese boxing world champion. The first time I experienced one of his fights was at one of the first Vale Tudo tournaments in Brazil where he was killing everyone.

At the end of the tournament, he fought in the best fight I had ever seen. He fought against Daniel Rego, who was my friend and training partner, and Marcelo had killed Daniel in that fight. Daniel's face was destroyed at the end, but he managed to get Giudici in a triangle to win the fight.

Surprisingly after that fight, when I came to train in São Paulo, he was there training with my cousin Ryan. What I like about Marcelo's game is that he brought a lot of Judo to our Jiu-Jitsu. He has very good pressure and was always ending up on top. He mixed the two styles very well and that made it an easy transition to Jiu-Jitsu.

From my point of view, he is one of the best coaches ever for MMA because of his background. He has a solid foundation in standup and his ability to transition from someone's guard or side control and keep the position while they're going for striking or for submissions was amazing. His top pressure was surprising to me when I first saw him fighting.

- Daniel Gracie

About Daniel Gracie

Born in Rio de Janeiro, Daniel Gracie has built a life full of achievements within the sport – whether in Jiu-Jitsu tournaments and competitions or in MMA events around the globe.

Daniel grew up in Rio De Janeiro in the same house as Robson, Renzo, Ryan, Ralph Gracie. Daniel has been immersed in Gracie Jiu-Jitsu for over 40 years.

He received his Black Belt from Carlos Gracie Jr. at age 23 and is currently a 6th Degree Gracie Brazilian Jiu-Jitsu Black Belt. Daniel has over 30 Gracie Jiu-Jitsu Academies / Affiliates around the world, 3000+ students and has trained hundreds of thousands of martial artists and influenced millions of others.

Some of Daniel Gracie's incredible accomplishments:

- 2X World Champion (IBJJF)

- 5X National Champion Brazil (IBJJF)

- 1X Pan Am Champion

- 8X State Champion (Rio De Janeiro Federation)

- Oscar of Jiu-Jitsu Champion (Super fight)

Marcelo Giudici

Professor Marcelo Giudici is an 5th degree Brazilian Jiu-Jitsu black belt under Ryan Gracie, 4th Degree Judo black belt, 7 tuen in Kung Fu, and black belt in Sanda.

Marcelo has 'Giudici Martial Arts' affiliate gyms around the world including Brazil, Argentina, Canada, Finland, Uruguay, Germany, Finland, China, Japan, Spain. He holds championship titles in Jiu-Jitsu, Sanda, and MMA.

Marcelo Giudici

MY EARLY LIFE

I grew up as an only child with my mother and father living in a poor neighborhood in São Paulo. Both of my parents worked very hard with my mother cleaning houses and my father working as a carpenter. My mother instilled discipline in me from a very young age and was the one who first introduced me to martial arts.

As a black belt in Judo, my mother taught me that martial arts was good for both mental and physical health and she wanted me to achieve this balance in my life. When I was 5 years old, she started bringing me with her to train Judo under Master Takahashi. She would work all week cleaning houses and train Judo with me on the weekend.

It was at this point in my life where I started to dedicate myself to martial arts. Growing up, when my friends would go to the park to play Fútbol after school I would take my gi, throw it over my back, and go to the gym. I achieved a high level of discipline very young in my life because my dream growing up was to become a black belt like my mother.

I never had any other job in my life; I would go to school, study, and train martial arts.

When I was 13, I began training Kung Fu (ying zhao). I continued training Judo under Master Takahashi but, like many others at that time, I was inspired to learn Kung Fu by Bruce Lee after watching him on television as 'Kato' in the Green Hornet show. I wanted to kick and fight like Bruce Lee, so I found an academy in São Paulo and began training Kung Fu under Master Li Win Kay.

I trained very hard in Kung Fu but after 2 to 3 years I could no longer afford to pay for my training. Master Li Win Kay and João Batista Soares offered me a job to continue my training; I could clean the dojo and begin teaching classes two times a week and that would be my payment.

After school I would go to the dojo, clean the bathrooms, sweep the mats, organize the equipment, and then teach and train in between. I would train Judo 3 days a week and Kung Fu 4 days with time for little else in-between. I learned so much from that experience and I look back at that time with pride knowing my true education came from the mat.

COMPETING

I loved to compete; my motivation was always to be the best fighter in every discipline. When I was 15, I began fighting in competitions and at 16, I traveled to China and became Champion of the World in Judo and Kung Fu. After winning, I began to find it difficult to stay motivated because techniques were limited in competition, and I wasn't learning anything new.

When I fought in Kung Fu, my father told me that I should wear gloves in competition. I told him Kung Fu as a discipline was more kicking and I would not be punching in competition. My father persisted in wanting me to wear gloves, so I put them on and after that fight he signed me up for boxing at Club Bank Commercial National (BCN) under coach Ralf Zurbano.

BCN Club was far from my home, and I had no other means of transportation other than a 45-minute bus ride into São Paulo. For 7 years, I would commute 2 to 3 times a week to train boxing; I will always be grateful to my father for pushing me because boxing helped round me out as a fighter. I developed a strong foundation in martial arts because I was cross-training in Judo, Kung Fu, and Boxing.

In 1995 I started fighting in the Brazilian form of mixed martial arts (MMA) called Vale Tudo. The first time I saw the sport, I said "wow, this is what I want to do". I began fighting in Vale Tudo Freestyle in São Paulo and started mixing the fighting disciplines I had learned with increased training and focus on Jiu-Jitsu.

Vale Tudo was a "no holds bar" way of fighting which meant no rules, you just needed to fight. The rounds were three, ten-minute

rounds with a minute rest. It was a tournament style competition where you needed to win 3 fights in one night to become champion. Back then you could kick the head to downed opponent, elbow, headbutt, everything.

I loved MMA because I believe it requires more strategy than other martial arts competitions. I had to balance conditioning with strong techniques; stand up, take downs, submissions, ground fighting. I knew that this was my place and I needed to be number one. I trained very hard, sometimes 6 or 8 hours a day, every day until I achieved my dream of becoming a Vale Tudo champion.

When I started fighting in Jiu-Jitsu people already knew my name from Vale Tudo and I felt the pressure to win. I knew I needed to train harder and take my Jiu-Jitsu training seriously because there were high expectations of me. I made a large impact on the world of Jiu-Jitsu, so much so that I caught the attention of the Gracie family.

Marcelo Giudici

Training with Ryan

I started training Jiu-Jitsu in Rio de Janeiro around 1986 when I was 20 years old. I stopped training in 1990 when I left Brazil to fight in the Chinese kickboxing competition known as Sanda. I competed in over 70 matches and became a 3-time world champion.

When MMA came to São Paulo around 1995, Ryan Gracie had already opened his Jiu-Jitsu academy "Gracie São Paulo". When I heard Ryan was teaching in São Paulo, I knew that's where I needed to train. I started making the one-hour commute from Campinas to São Paulo to train with Ryan 2 to 3 times a week for 12 years until his passing in 2007.

Ryan was very young when he opened his gym in São Paulo, and he attracted a lot of younger fighters. I was 29 and already a purple belt when I began training with him. His style of fighting was reflected in his training; intense, aggressive, and lots of pressure. Ryan was very direct which many people did not like but was perfect for me.

Ryan's coaching style was much different than what most people experience today when training Jiu-Jitsu. Not every person who trained at Gracie São Paulo loved Jiu-Jitsu, but we all loved Ryan, so we came together and united around him.

The people who left, left because the training was too hard. The people who stayed, stayed for Ryan.

I loved the gym and the people I trained with, which included some great Jiu-Jitsu practitioners; Mauricio Alonso, Gabriel Vella, Daniel Gracie, and Carlos Russo.

I have always had this passion to push myself to work harder than anyone else. I needed to prove to myself that I could be the best and, although I loved the people I trained with, I always had a desire to prove myself in any martial arts I trained. In Jiu-Jitsu, I knew I needed to invest more into my training, so I started paying for private lessons two times a week for six years.

In those six years I stayed a purple belt and was the last of my friends to receive my brown belt. I never asked Ryan "why not me" when I saw my friends being promoted because I knew my belt would come once I proved myself on the mat.

I had to invest more into my training because I was the smallest guy at the gym. The other guys were bigger, taller, stronger, and would smash me every time we trained. I knew my size would hold me back, so I needed to develop stronger techniques to make up for my lack of size and strength.

A lot of my success in Jiu-Jitsu came from my training with Ryan but most of all it was because of those friends who would smash me every day in training. My friends helped push me to grow my techniques and taught me that I needed to develop stronger defense and learn how to counter bigger opponents.

I believe that when you have good defense in Jiu-Jitsu you further develop your attacks because you can anticipate what your opponent is going to do before they do it. I studied the different ways my opponent would try to escape, learn how to block their escape, and how to counter with a submission.

I knew I was fully embraced by Ryan as part of his team when he told me I could get the tattoo of the gym. I saw other people have

the tattoo and I wanted to be accepted as one of his top fighters. Immediately after Ryan telling me I went out and got my tattoo on my right arm on my inner bicep. The right arm represents the right side of the Gracie family and my Jiu-Jitsu lineage under Ryan.

In Jiu-Jitsu, I was in the top ten fighters at Gracie São Paulo, but in MMA I was number one.

In Brazil there was Jiu-Jitsu and Luta Livre, and these two disciplines were also at odds with each other to prove what style was the best. Luta Livre was the Brazilian form of wrestling and different from Jiu-Jitsu in that their style of fighting was trained without a gi.

Luta Livre fighters would challenge us all the time so we would close the gym, lock the doors and we would fight to prove who was the best. I had a lot of fights because of this rivalry and our philosophy was we would fight, and at the end the winner would be the one who opened the door.

After Ryan died, it was just never the same. I was very sad after he passed, and after talking with his family I decided I needed space from the gym. Whenever people talk about Ryan Gracie, I still feel the connection and will come to his defense after all these years.

NEW CHALLENGES

It didn't matter if I was living in Brazil or fighting in another country. I would come to the defense of our gym and defend the Gracie family from anyone who criticized them.

My most important challenge came from Eugenio Tadeu; I was proud to fight him, because he was a very famous Luta Livre fighter in Vale Tudo. I trained so hard for my fight with Eugenio and after I won, his fame helped grow my name in Vale Tudo.

After my fight with Eugenio, I traveled the world to fight in martial arts competitions in the United States, Japan, China, Finland, Russia, and other countries. At that time in my life, my name was growing, and I began opening my gyms.

There are now "Giudici Brazilian Jiu-Jitsu" gyms in 12 countries around the world with my first affiliation starting with my good friend Pablo Lucero in Argentina. Around 1995 I began traveling to Argentina and now I go back every year, three times a year to give seminars. Pablo Lucero has done great work in Argentina making Giudici Brazilian Jiu-Jitsu number one in MMA and Jiu-Jitsu.

Professor Marcelo Giudici, Grand Master Robson Gracie, and Master Renzo Gracie

I'VE GIVEN MY LIFE TO THE MAT

BENEFITS

My opinion is that Jiu-Jitsu is number one for self-defense and continues to be the best martial art in the world because of its effectiveness. The Gracie's proved that Brazilian Jiu-Jitsu is the best martial arts in the world when Rorion Gracie brought Jiu-Jitsu to the United States in 1993.

I have fought against and practiced several different martial arts from around the world including; Karate, Kung Fu, Boxing, Tae Kwon Do, Sambo, Wrestling, and Sanda. In my experience, Jiu-Jitsu has the most effective techniques when fighting against those other martial arts disciplines.

Jiu-Jitsu is not only about techniques but also a balance of emotion and building strong confidence. Jiu-Jitsu isn't about mountains and the oceans, that's for yoga, my philosophy for Jiu-Jitsu is to build confidence. Jiu-Jitsu is about "I'm a small guy, but I can beat a big guy."

I myself, am not a big guy with big muscles but my mind is strong because I believe in my Jiu-Jitsu techniques. When I taught in Russia, these big strong guys would come to the gym and challenge me to prove that Sambo was the best. I would win those fights because I believed in my techniques and because I was not intimidated by bigger fighters.

I believe the more you train the more confidence you will have. If I did not have that then I would not have been able to control these bigger, stronger fighters. With more training, you can control yourself and control your emotions.

BJJ Philosophy

I remember one student I had didn't even want to leave his room or go to school because he was so afraid of being bullied. After training Jiu-Jitsu with me he began to walk outside with his head held high with the confidence that Jiu-Jitsu has given him.

Jiu-Jitsu isn't only about being champion of the world, it is about building good character, confidence, and becoming a good person in the future.

I have seen how a country's culture can influence the type of students I receive in the gym. For a gym to be strong, I need discipline, attention, and I need my students to build confidence. Technique and building the body is the easy part, building confidence and controlling your emotions is the hardest for most people to learn.

Building your mental toughness will be something you will need throughout your life and is something that Jiu-Jitsu can give you. In every martial arts, you need to balance your life between physical and mental training. In life, you will have ups and downs, but your ups need to exceed your downs so that you are still progressing in your life. Your life should be like stairs with each step making you a stronger person.

You might be champion of the world and you will be tapped; the difference is that mental strength and confidence will tell you that "today I tapped to you, tomorrow you will tap to me." That is what Jiu-Jitsu can give to you.

MODERN Jiu-Jitsu

Growing up, Jiu-Jitsu was about pride in your gym, and you would give 100% to represent your gym. When you arrived as a black belt, you were a true black belt. You earned it through the challenges the gyms demanded of you. Myself and others who are now considered "old school" remember the pride you felt when receiving your black belt because we knew we had achieved something great.

Today, there are a lot of black belts who only care about the techniques. They base their Jiu-Jitsu philosophy on how many techniques they know and not about upholding the traditions of Jiu-Jitsu. Many schools I've seen do not have students who bow before getting onto the mat.

Bowing represents giving yourself to the mat and leaving your ego behind.

These gyms do not focus on discipline or philosophy of Jiu-Jitsu, just the techniques. The biggest problem in Jiu-Jitsu today is that everyone craves the status of having a black belt. The black belt is not a status, it should represent the knowledge you've achieved and the desire to learn more. The difference between white and black belts is the ability and knowledge they've achieved in Jiu-Jitsu.

Black belts should be growing Jiu-Jitsu in their communities and spreading the philosophy that it represents and not just taking money from their students. These people only crave the status of being a black belt but do not care about its history.

BJJ Philosophy

Some of these black belts earn their belts in a short amount of time, 4-5 years, and never learn what it means to struggle and grind to prove themselves like we had to. I waited 6 years as a purple belt, 10-11 years to achieve my black belt.

Being a black belt is like going to a university, you need to continue to study Jiu-Jitsu. I am a five-degree black belt and I still talk with friends about techniques and the progress of Jiu-Jitsu because martial arts are always growing and evolving.

New black belts today think that once they get their belt, they can teach the class or open their own gym.

I have a strict philosophy when I promote someone to a black belt: 1) are they going to be faithful to the gym, 2) do they demonstrate good character, 3) are they a good role model for other students, 4) and then do they have good techniques.

Today, there are so many "YouTube" black belts who focus on learning and demonstrating their techniques but lack the discipline and culture that can only be earned on the mat. The Jiu-Jitsu philosophy and respect for the mat are what's most important to me.

CHOOSING A GYM

People now and days can use the internet to learn techniques and progress through the belt system. Before joining a Jiu-Jitsu gym, look at the registration and certifications of the owner or instructor. Take their name and ask other black belts around the world. The world of Jiu-Jitsu is big, but at the same time it is also a small community. Check who gave them their black belt, do your research, and check their credentials.

One example in Finland, one black belt I met said he was a Jiu-Jitsu world champion and when I checked with the other black belts, they said he was lying. He was in Brazil as a purple belt and when he left, he suddenly became a two-degree black belt. These people only want to take advantage of the lack of information available between the different countries which makes it difficult to prove who they are or what they've achieved.

Unfortunately, there are so many fake black belts who were blue or purple belts and want to teach or open their gym, so they give themselves a black belt, without having truly earned it.

Taking classes, hearing what they're talking about, along their philosophy and discipline on the mat will tell you everything you need to know.

RYAN
GRACIE

45

Passing Half Guard

Passing Half Guard - Variation 1

1. With your LEFT arm, hug the head, grip their LEFT shoulder, and apply pressure down. You need to apply pressure to your opponent by pushing your LEFT knee against their hip/thigh.

2. Turn your hips and begin walking your foot up as high as you can while applying pressure. When starting to pass, your leg should NOT be **stretched** out. Bring your knee up and plant your foot flat on the mat.

3. Grip the pants and push the leg down and away from you until it passes your knee.

4. Turn your hips, bring your knee up and slice across their leg. Control your opponent's LEFT arm as your free your leg. From step 1 to 5, hug around the opponent's head and grip the shoulder to maintain control and prevent them from posturing up or creating space.

5. Pull the opponent's LEFT arm as you bring your knee down, scoot your body up further onto their chest into mount position. From steps 4 to 5, control your opponent's arm on the side of the trapped leg to prevent them from blocking your knee when moving to mount.

6. As you pass, continue to scoot forward bringing your knees deeper into their armpits with hands out for stability.

Application

When in half guard, it is important to know where you need to be to maintain control of your opponent so you can pass effectively.

Throughout this variation you'll need to remember to

maintain control of your opponent's neck by gripping their shoulder. Second, you cannot keep your trapped leg extended as you'll open yourself up to potential leg locks which will be covered in a later section. So, keep your foot planted on the mat and maintain as many points of contacts as possible.

1

With your LEFT arm, hug the head, grip their LEFT shoulder, and apply downward shoulder pressure.

2

Turn your hips and begin walking your foot up as high as you can while applying pressure.

Important Details

1.A - You need to apply pressure to your opponent by pushing your LEFT knee against their hip/thigh.

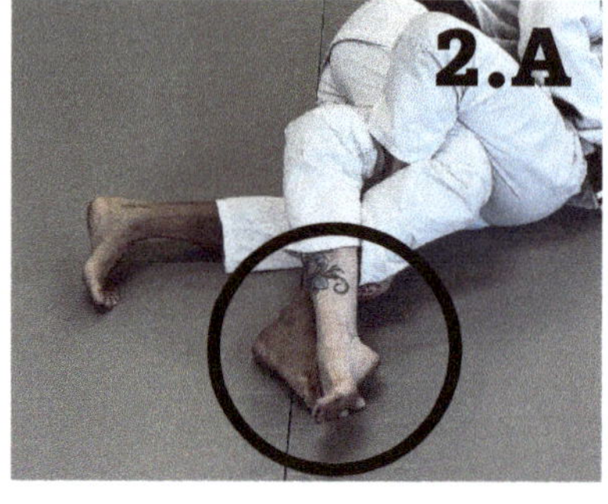

2.A - When starting to pass, your leg should NOT be **stretched** out. Bring your knee up and plant your foot flat on the mat.

3

Grip the pants and push the leg down and away from you until it passes your knee.

4

Turn your hips, bring your knee up and slice across their leg. Control your opponent's LEFT arm and free your leg.

Important Details

4.A - From step 1 to 5, hug around the opponent's head and grip the shoulder to maintain control and prevent them from posturing up or creating space.

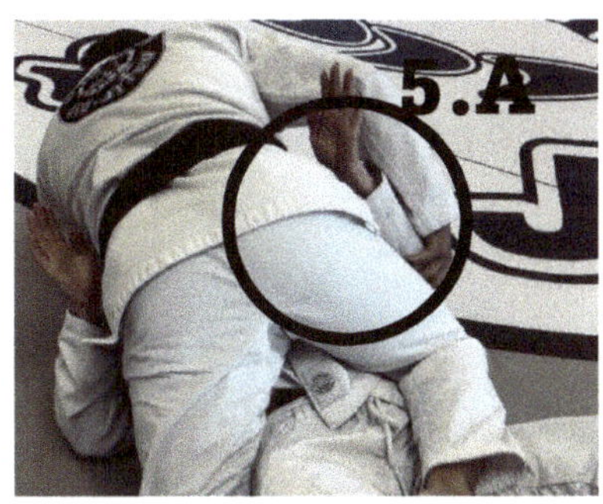

5.A - From steps 4 to 5, control your opponent's arm on the side of the trapped leg to prevent them from blocking your knee when moving to mount.

5

Pull their LEFT arm as you bring your knee down, scoot your body up further onto their chest into mount position.

6

As you pass, continue to scoot forward bringing your knees deeper into their armpits with hands out for stability.

1. Switch your grip from LEFT to RIGHT by sliding your hand under you're their head and gripping their LEFT shoulder.

2. Bring your head down towards the mat on the opposite side of your opponent's head and come up onto your toes.

3. Take a big step backward with your LEFT leg while maintaining control of your opponent's neck and shoulder.

4. Once on the other side, post out your leg and scoot backward toward your opponent's shoulder to free your leg. Taking a big step prevents your leg from being trapped into full guard. Post your foot out for stability and it provides a base, so you're not rolled. Grip the pants to maintain control of your opponent and stop them from hip escaping until you're ready to step back over to the other side.

5. With your LEFT hand, open your opponent's gi and pass their lapel under to your RIGHT hand under their shoulder. Locking your opponent's shoulder with their lapel stops them from rolling towards you and from pushing you up/away to prevent you from passing.

6. Feed the lapel into your RIGHT hand, cinch it until you have a tight grip and effectively locking your opponent's shoulder. A two fingered grip is very common in Jiu-Jitsu and can be used to create a tighter grip.

7. Reach across your opponent with your LEFT hand and take a big step with your LEFT leg stepping back over to their RIGHT side. Be mindful of your opponent's hands which may come up to block you

8. Turn your RIGHT knee down to the RIGHT and continue to grip your opponent's shoulder with your RIGHT hand. When stepping across, maintain your grip on your opponent's shoulder and apply downward pressure.

9. As you're coming down, turn your hips in towards your opponent and bring your RIGHT knee to the mat for stability. You will need to take a big step to clear your opponent's legs and prevent them opening their legs and pulling you into closed guard.

10. As you pass, continue to scoot forward bringing your knees deeper into their armpits with hands out for stability. When sitting into mount, your foot/ankle may still be stuck. Scoot forward onto your opponent's chest to free your foot without posturing up.

Application

To perform this variation, you will need to have the ability to jump over your opponent which will require practice.

In the later section, we will discuss a drill that is aimed at developing

this skill. This technique is useful when your opponent has a strong lockdown on your leg, and you are unable to pull it free.

Some opponents are focused on keeping your leg locked rather than regaining guard, this variation will need to be timed when you feel you have your control points in place.

1

Switch your grip from LEFT to RIGHT by sliding your hand under you're their head and gripping their LEFT shoulder.

2

Bring your head down towards the mat on the opposite side of your opponent's head and come up onto your toes.

Important Details

4.A - Taking a big step prevents your leg from being trapped into full guard. Post your foot out for stability as it provides a base, so you're not rolled.

4.B - Grip the pants to maintain control of your opponent and stop them from hip escaping until you're ready to step back over to the other side.

3

Take a big step backward with your LEFT leg while maintaining control of your opponent's neck and shoulder.

4

Once on the other side, post out your leg and scoot backward toward their shoulder to free your leg.

Alternate Technique

5.A - Locking your opponent's shoulder with their lapel stops them from rolling towards you and from pushing you up/away to prevent you from passing.

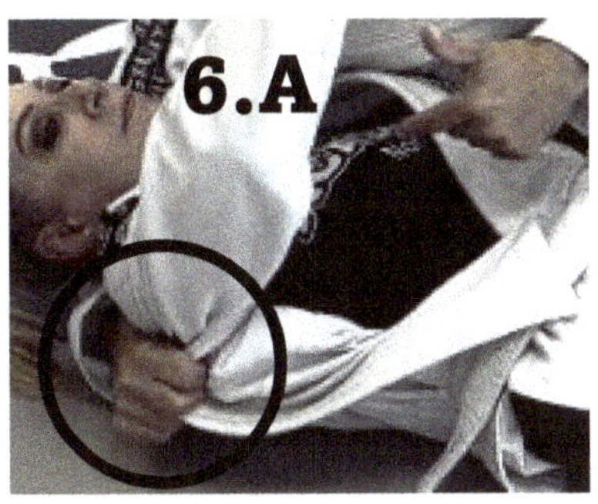

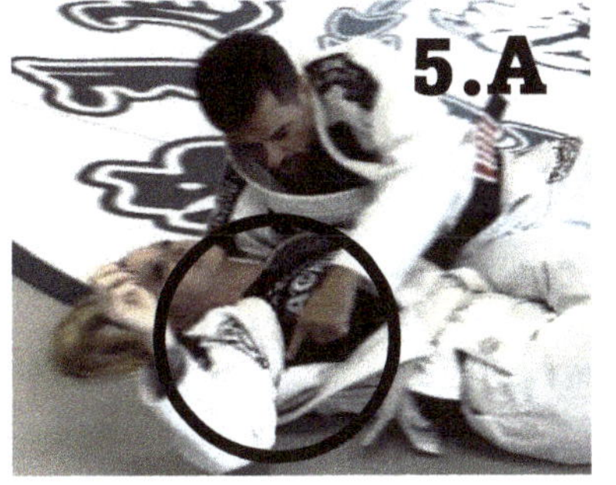

6.A - A two fingered grip is very common in Jiu-Jitsu and can be used to create a tighter grip in smaller spaces.

5

With your LEFT hand, open your opponent's gi and pass their lapel to your RIGHT hand under their shoulder.

6

Feed the lapel into your RIGHT hand and pull it tight to effectively lock your opponent's shoulder.

Important Details

7.A - Be mindful of your opponents hands which may come up to block you if you did not lock their shoulders.

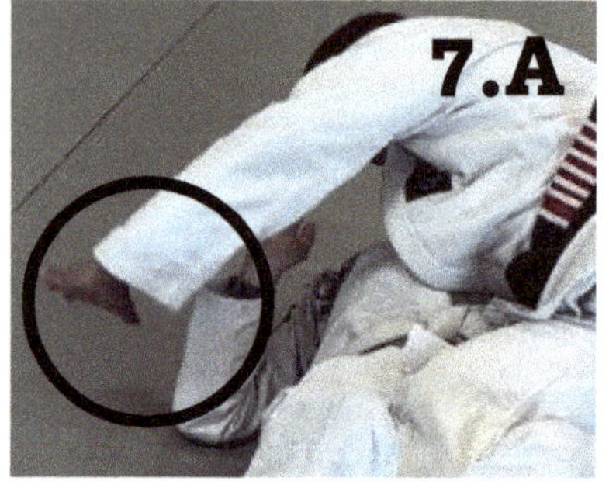

8.A - When stepping across, maintain your grip on your opponent's shoulder and apply downward pressure.

7

Reach across with your LEFT hand and take a big step with your LEFT leg stepping back over to their RIGHT side.

8

Turn your RIGHT knee down to the RIGHT and continue to grip your opponents shoulder with your RIGHT hand.

Important Details

9.A - You will need to take a big step to clear your opponent's legs and prevent them opening their legs and pulling you into closed guard.

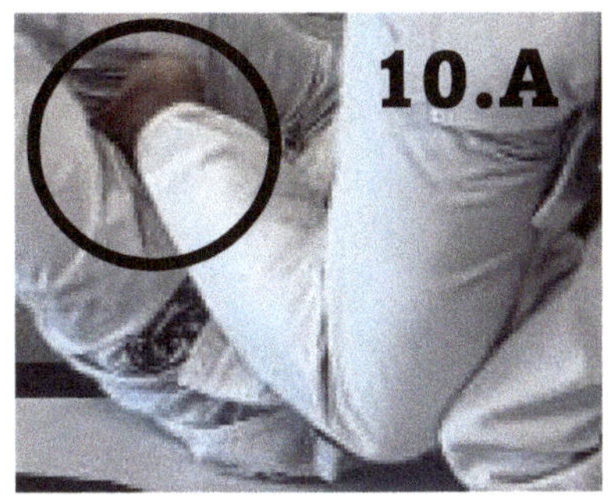

10.A - When sitting into mount, your foot/ankle may still be stuck. Scoot forward onto your opponent's chest to free your foot without posturing up.

9

As you're coming down, turn your hips inward and bring your RIGHT knee to the mat for stability.

10

As you pass, continue to scoot forward bringing your knees deeper into their armpits with hands out for stability.

Passing from Half Guard to SIDE CONTROL

Hon Kesa Gatame

100 Kilos

1. As you start to pass, bring your RIGHT hand under their arm hooking the right shoulder and gripping their collar. Maintain pressure against their head with your head down on the mat.

2. Your head will come down, touching the mat and turned away, on the opposite side of your opponent's head. From steps 2 to 8, maintain your grip on the collar with your RIGHT hand and apply downward pressure with your shoulder onto the chest.

3. Come off your knees and lift your butt up into the air using both feet while applying downward pressure.

4. Plant your LEFT hand down for support and take a big step out with your LEFT leg.

5. Keeping your head down and against your opponent, hop your feet forward on your toes until your knee is free. Continue to hop forward until you feel your knee has completely passed the line of your opponent's thigh.

6. Turn your RIGHT knee in towards your LEFT leg, slide it out until your knee is down and touching the mat. Maintain pressure down and weight towards the knee. If your body is too high, it will cause you to become unbalanced and rolled over.

7. Keeping your knee down on the mat, with your LEFT foot push against your opponent's leg to free your foot. Your foot needs to be against the opponent's knee and pushed against simultaneously as you are pulling your leg out.

8. Once your leg is free keep it tucked in tight while applying downward pressure and grip your opponent's RIGHT elbow. Grip the arm near the elbow and raise it up as you bring your knee down. Trapping the arm prevents them from blocking your knee as you pass.

9.   Pull the elbow and slide your knee across the mat, bringing your RIGHT knee near the head, and sit into hon kesa gatame. Create space for your leg by raising your body up with your LEFT leg, slide your RIGHT knee out and sit back down into hon kesa gatame.

10. Sit perpendicular to your opponent with your knee near the head and the other foot planted on the mat for stability. Grip the shoulder under the arm with your RIGHT hand and control the elbow with your LEFT hand.

Application

In this variation, you will need to to maintain downward pressure on your opponent using two control elements; your head and the underhook.

When entering half guard you will need to first establish your underhook on the opposite side of your trapped leg. This will also help prevent an opponent from trying to take your back.

Use your head to push your opponent's face away from you to prevent them from effectively using their hip escape.

1

As you start to pass, bring your RIGHT hand under their arm hooking the right shoulder and gripping their collar.

2

Your head will come down, touching the mat and turned away, on the opposite side of your opponent's head.

Important Details

1.A - Use your head to apply pressure against your opponent's head. Maintain pressure against their head with your head down on the mat.

2.A - From steps 2 to 8, maintain your grip on the collar with your RIGHT hand and apply downward pressure with your shoulder onto the chest.

3

Come off your knees and lift your butt up into the air using both feet while applying downward pressure.

4

Plant your LEFT hand down for support and take a big step out with your LEFT leg.

Important Details

5.A - Continue to hop forward until you feel your knee has completely passed the line of your opponent's thighs.

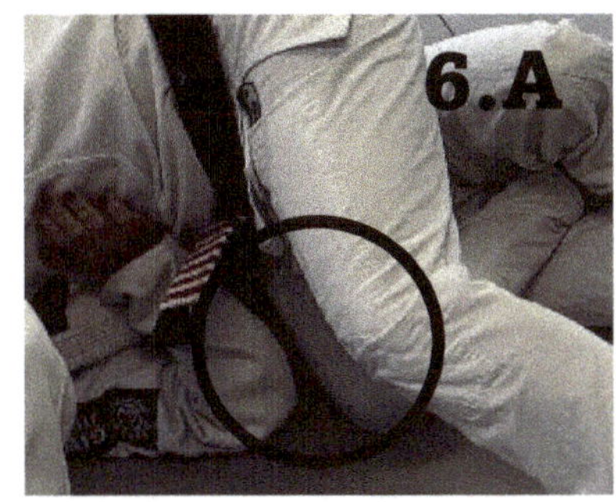

6.A - Maintain pressure down and weight towards the knee. If your body is too high, it will cause you to become unbalanced and rolled over.

5

Keeping your head down and against your opponent, hop your feet forward on your toes until your knee is free.

6

Turn your RIGHT knee in towards your LEFT leg, slide it out until your knee is down and touching the mat.

Important Details

7.A - Your foot needs to be against the opponent's knee and pushed against simultaneously as you are pulling your leg out.

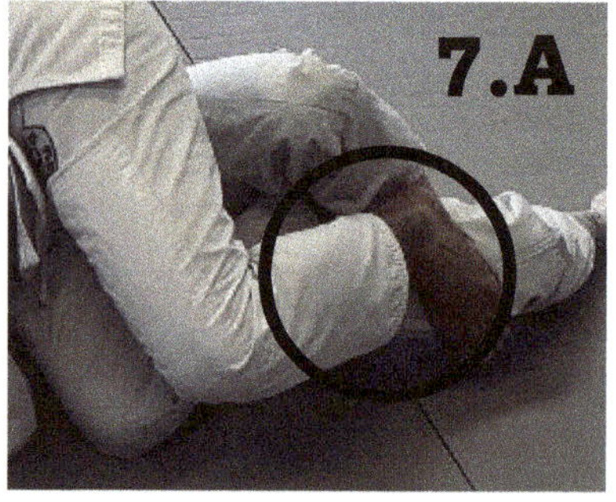

8.A - Grip the arm near the elbow and raise it up as you bring your knee down. Trap the arm to prevent them from blocking your knee as you pass.

7

Keeping your knee down on the mat, with your LEFT foot push against your opponent's leg to free your foot.

8

Once your leg is free keep it tucked in tight while applying downward pressure and grip your opponent's RIGHT elbow.

Important Details

9.A - Create space for your leg by raising your body up with your LEFT leg, slide your RIGHT knee out and sit back down into hon kesa gatame.

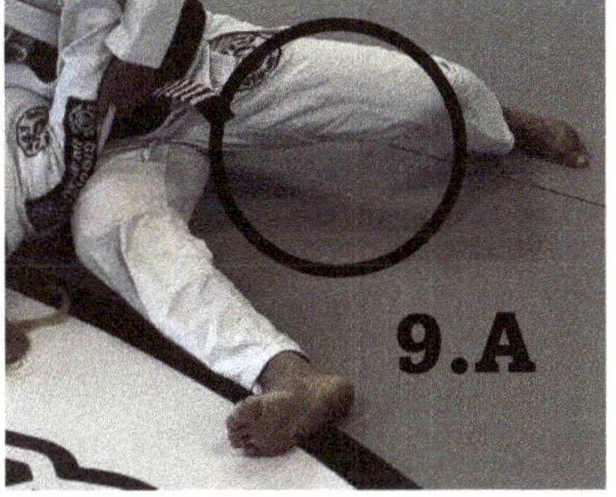

10.A - Continue to grip the shoulder under the arm with your RIGHT hand and control the elbow with your LEFT hand.

9

Pull the elbow and slide your RIGHT knee across the mat towards the opponent's head and sit into hon kesa gatame.

10

Sit perpendicular to your opponent with your knee near the head and the other foot planted on the mat for stability.

1. Bring both of your hands under your opponent's arms hooking their shoulders and gripping the collar from both sides. Locking the shoulder prevents your opponent from blocking your knee from sliding up when trying to pass.

2. Open your elbows, your weight comes down onto their chest, as you bring your head down to the mat and apply pressure. Trapping both arms means your opponent cannot hip escape to their right or create space by pushing on your shoulder.

3. Come off your knees and lift your butt up into the air using both feet while applying downward pressure.

4. Keep both arms locked on their shoulders, open your elbows for stability, and take a big step out with your LEFT leg.

5. Keeping your head down and against your opponent, hop your feet forward on your toes until your knee is free. Continue to hop forward until you feel your knee has completely passed the line of your opponent's thigh.

6. Turn your RIGHT knee in towards your LEFT leg, slide it out until your knee is down and touching the mat. Maintain pressure down and weight towards the knee. If your body is too high, it will cause you to become unbalanced and rolled over.

7. Keeping your knee down on the mat, with your LEFT foot push against your opponent's leg to free your foot. Your foot needs to be against the opponent's knee and pushed against simultaneously as you are pulling your leg out.

8. Once your leg is free, tuck it in tight while applying downward pressure and raise your opponent's RIGHT shoulder. Continue to grip the shoulder and raise it up as you bring your knee down. Trap the arm to prevent them from blocking your knee as you pass.

9. Lift the shoulder and slide your knee across the mat, bringing your RIGHT knee near the head, and sit into hon kesa gatame. With your under-arm grip on the shoulder raise their RIGHT arm up, tuck your knee in, and sit into hon kesa gatame.

10. Continue to grip the shoulder under the arm with your LEFT hand, raise them up, and transition to 100 kilos. As you switch your position, pull up on the RIGHT shoulder and tuck your knee under for more control.

JIU-JITSU

Application

Similar to variation 3, you will need to maintain control of your opponent so you can pass effectively.

In this variation, you will be locking both of your opponent's shoulders for added control. You will need to establish and maintain two underhooks on your opponent while continuing to utilize your head to turn their neck, making them look away.

An important point to remember is using your elbows for stability and awareness of the potential to be rolled by your opponent.

1

Bring both of your hands under your opponent's arms hooking their shoulders and gripping the collar from both sides.

2

Open your elbows, your weight comes down onto their chest, as you bring your head down to the mat and apply pressure.

Important Details

1.A - Locking the shoulder prevents your opponent from blocking your knee from sliding up when trying to pass.

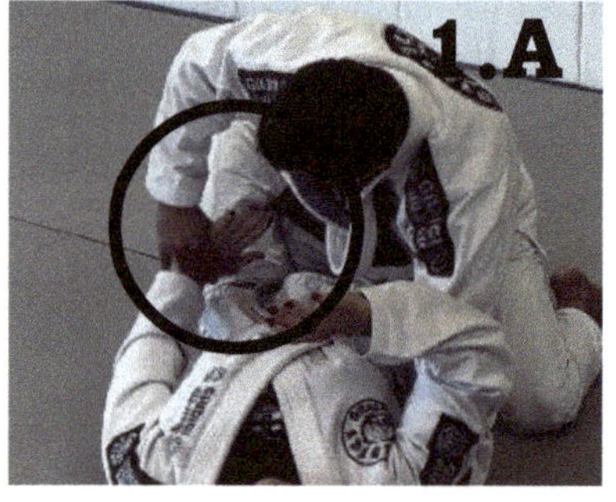

2.A - Trapping both arms means your opponent cannot hip escape to their right or create space by pushing on your shoulder.

3

Come off your knees and lift your butt up into the air using both feet while applying downward pressure.

4

Keep both arms locked on their shoulders, open your elbows for stability, and take a step out with your LEFT leg.

Important Details

5.A - Continue to hop forward until you feel your knee has completely passed the line of your opponent's thighs.

6.A - Maintain pressure down and weight towards the knee. If your body is too high, it will cause you to become unbalanced and rolled over.

5

Keeping your head down and against your opponent, hop your feet forward on your toes until your knee is free.

6

Turn your RIGHT knee in towards your LEFT leg, slide it out until your knee is down and touching the mat.

Important Details

7.A - Your foot needs to be against the opponent's knee and pushed against simultaneously as you are pulling your leg out.

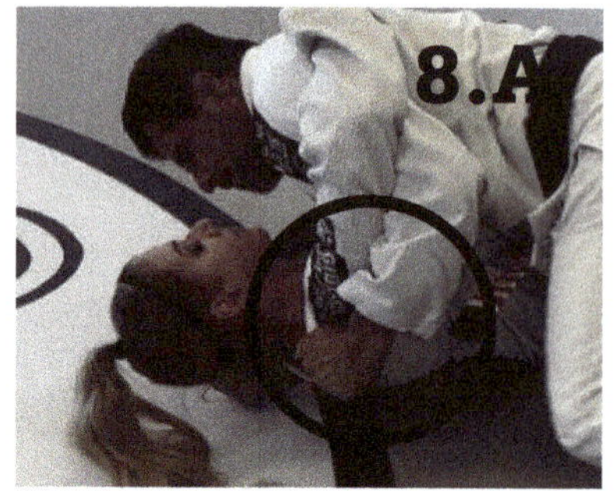

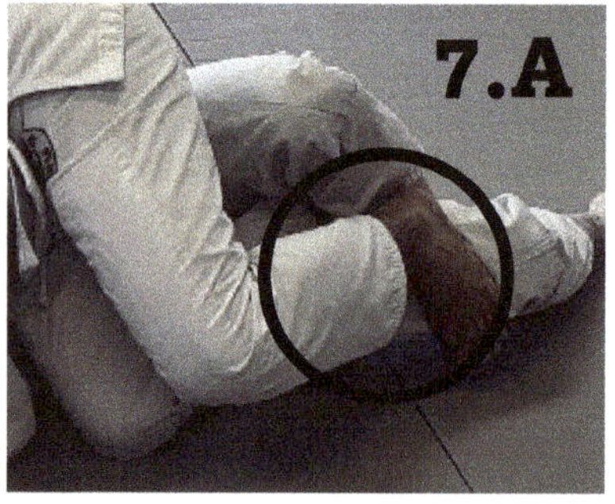

8.A - Continue to grip the shoulder and raise it up as you bring your knee down. Trap the arm to prevent them from blocking your knee as you pass.

7

Keeping your knee down on the mat, with your LEFT foot push against your opponent's leg to free your foot.

8

Once your leg is free, tuck it in tight while applying downward pressure and raise your opponent's RIGHT shoulder.

Important Details

9.A - With your under arm grip on the shoulder raise their RIGHT arm up, tuck your knee in, and sit into hon kesa gatame.

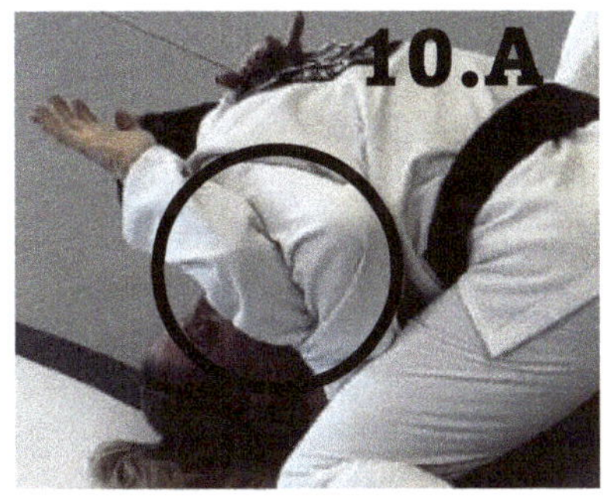

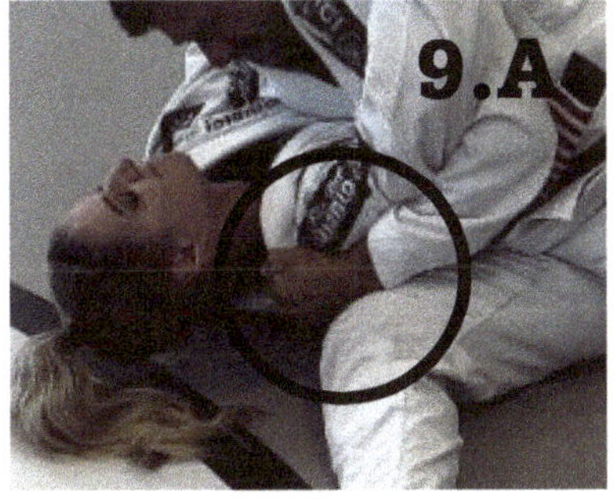

10.A - As you switch your position, pull up on the RIGHT shoulder and tuck your knee under for more control.

9

Pull the elbow and slide your RIGHT knee across the mat towards the opponent's head and sit into hon kesa gatame.

10

Continue to grip the shoulder under the arm with your LEFT hand, raise them up, and transition to 100 kilos.

1. When you feel your opponent initiate the calf lock and start to extend you need to react quickly or you will tap.

2. As your opponent secures the calf lock, keep your head down and scoot your body back until your knees are past 90 degrees. When scooting back you will need to bring your shoulders past their belt line while keeping your head down and applying pressure.

3. As you're scooting back, reach under and hug your opponent's legs by gripping your hands at or below their butt. Once you are in position, lock your hands under the legs and squeeze. The tighter you lock your hands the more effective this technique will be.

4. With your hands secured under your opponent, extend your trapped leg back until you break the lock on your leg.

5. Sprawl out your legs onto your toes and keep your weight down onto your opponent. As you sprawl, keep your weight forward on your opponent by coming up on your toes and knees off the mat.

6. Transition your grip by releasing the legs and grabbing onto the belt with both hands on either side of your opponent. Gripping the belt is preferred but if the opponent's belt came off then you can grip the pants or the gi.

7. Take a big step out and walk your legs to the LEFT side of your opponent and bring them together while applying pressure. Keep your weight forward on your opponent by coming up on your toes and walk your legs around without touching your knees to the mat. Throughout the pass, keep your head down and your weight forward against your opponent.

8. Lift your hips up and slide your RIGHT knee across the mat into hon kesa gatame side control position.

9. Use your LEFT hand to grip the collar and your RIGHT hand comes under to grip their shoulder as you scoot forward. Griping the collar prevents your opponent from pushing you backward and it helps you scoot forward as you sit into hon kesa gatame.

10. Grip their RIGHT elbow, turn your body and sit into 100 kilos side control position. As you switch your position, lift their RIGHT shoulder and tuck your knee under for more control.

Application

For this variation, we will focus on escaping the lockdown on your leg and preventing a submission caused by the calf lock.

This is an effective position for your opponent as you move into half guard because they will keep control of your leg and are capable of submitting you from their half guard.

Even without the threat of submission, this technique will also help escaping half guard when an opponent is pushing down on your head which prevents you from executing other techniques.

1

When you feel your opponent initiate the calf lock and start to extend you need to react quickly.

2

When you feel the calf lock, keep your head down and scoot back until your knees are past 90 degrees.

Important Details

2.A - When scooting back you will need to bring your shoulders past their belt line while keeping your head down and applying pressure.

3.A - Once you are in position, lock your hands under the legs and squeeze. The tighter you lock your hands the more effective this technique will be.

3

As you're scooting back, reach under and hug their legs by gripping your hands at or below their butt.

4

With your hands secured under your opponent, extend your trapped leg back until you break the lock on your leg.

Important Details

5.A - As you sprawl, keep your weight forward on your opponent by coming up on your toes and knees off the mat.

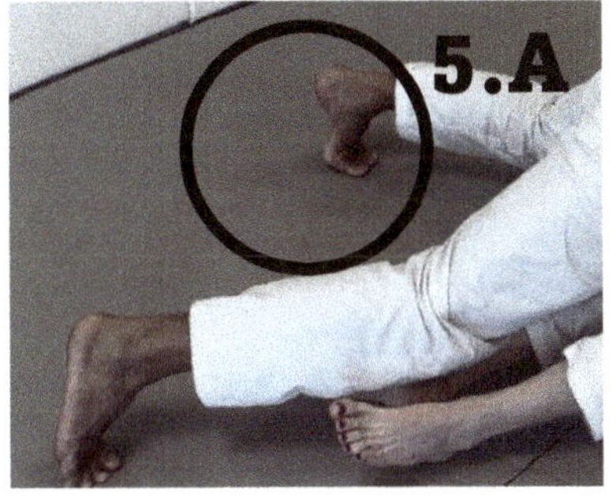

6.A - Gripping the belt is preferred but if the opponent's belt came off then you can grip the pants or the gi.

5

Sprawl out your legs onto your toes and keep your weight down onto your opponent.

6

Transition your grip by releasing the legs and grabbing onto the belt with both hands on each side of your opponent.

Important Details

7.A - Keep your weight forward on your opponent by coming up on your toes and walk your legs around without touching your knees to the mat.

7.B - Throughout the pass, keep your head down and your weight forward against your opponent.

7

Take a big step out and walk your legs to the LEFT side of your opponent while applying downward pressure.

8

Lift your hips up and slide your RIGHT knee across the mat into hon kesa gatame side control position.

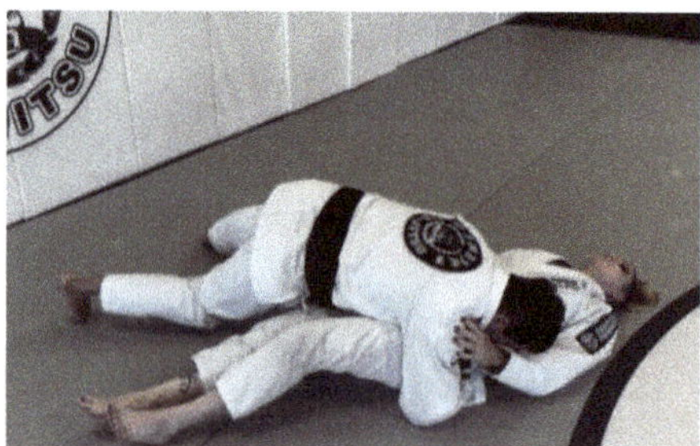

Important Details

9.A - Griping the collar prevents your opponent from pushing you backward and it helps you scoot forward as you sit into hon kesa gatame.

10.A - As you switch your position, lift up their RIGHT shoulder and tuck your knee under for more control.

9

Use your LEFT hand to grip the collar and your RIGHT hand comes under to grip their shoulder as you scoot forward.

10

Grip their RIGHT elbow, turn your body and sit into 100 kilos side control position.

85

1. Shift your hips with your weight down to your knees, lock your legs around your opponent's leg into a triangle .

2. Reach under your opponent's head and arm with your RIGHT hand and grip their LEFT shoulder. If you have the flexibility, you can lock your legs into a triangle OR you can hook your opponent's leg and apply pressure with just your foot.

3. Push up your opponent's arm with your LEFT hand to create space where you will be rolling.

4. Bring your RIGHT hand over and reach under your body as you lift your legs and push off the mat into a forward roll. This movement needs to be quick as your whole body needs to reach under and initiate the roll by pushing off the mat with both feet.

5. As you initiate the roll, with your LEFT hand, reach down and grip the opponent's RIGHT knee. Keep pressure on your RIGHT leg against your opponent and use that leg as the primary source of momentum for the roll.

6. Turn your RIGHT knee in towards your LEFT leg, slide it out until your knee is down and touching the mat. Use both hands to push your opponent to the other side and control where they land once the pass is complete.

7. Control the hips throughout the roll and reach over to grip your opponent's shoulder to stop from rolling away. You need to continue the momentum to posture up and reach under your opponent's arm. Do not stop and wait or your opponent will escape.

8. Grip the opponent's shoulder or collar and pull them into back mount and immediately get your hooks in with both legs. When securing your opponent', use your LEFT hand to open the collar and place your RIGHT hand deep inside across their neck and grip the collar.

9. As you get your hooks in, immediately reach over and under with both hands into the seatbelt position.

10. Extend your legs and pull backward with your arms to stretch out your opponent. When getting your grips, use one hand to grip the collar and the other to come under your opponent's arm and grip their wrist for more control. When getting hooks, your ankles should not be crossed as it could lead to a submission and failure to get points in a competition.

JIU-JITSU

Application

These next variations will focus on taking your opponent's back.

As with the jumping variation, this will require practice and abilities as you perform your forward roll to pass their half guard. Keep in mind the space needed to perform the roll and where your opponent's body is positioned. If they are crunched to the same side trying to hip escape the roll won't be effective.

Another consideration is how much they are locking down your leg because if it's too loose then your roll won't work as intended.

1

Shift your hips with your weight down to your knees, lock your legs around your opponent's leg into a triangle .

2

Reach under your opponent's head and arm with your RIGHT hand and grip their LEFT shoulder.

Important Details

2.A - If you have the flexibility, you can lock your legs into a triangle OR you can hook your opponent's leg and apply pressure with just your foot.

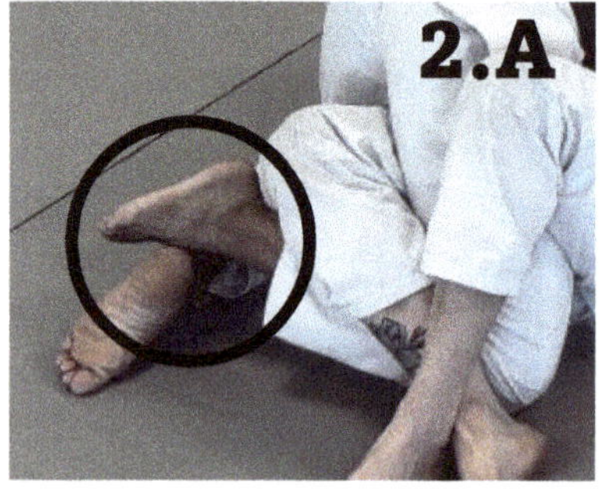

4.A - This movement needs to be quick as your whole body needs to reach under and initiate the roll by pushing off the mat with both feet.

3

Push up your opponent's arm with your LEFT hand to create space where you will be rolling.

4

Bring your RIGHT hand over and reach under your body as you lift your legs and push off the mat into a forward roll.

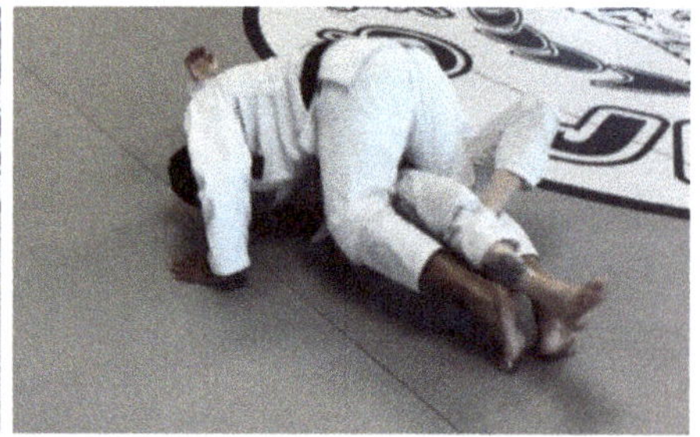

Important Details

5.A - Keep pressure on your RIGHT leg against your opponent and use that leg as the primary source of momentum for the roll.

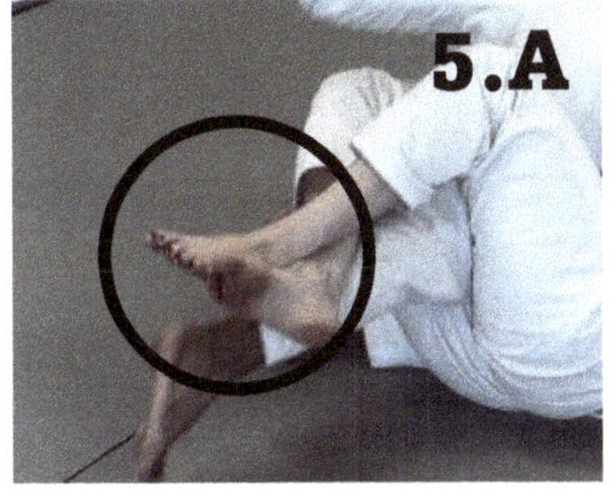

6.A - Use both hands to push your opponent to the other side and control where they land once the pass is complete.

5

As you initiate the roll, with your LEFT hand, reach down and grip the opponent's RIGHT knee.

6

Turn your RIGHT knee in towards your LEFT leg, slide it out until your knee is down and touching the mat.

Important Details

7.A - You need to continue the momentum to posture up and reach under your opponent's arm. Do not stop and wait or your opponent will escape.

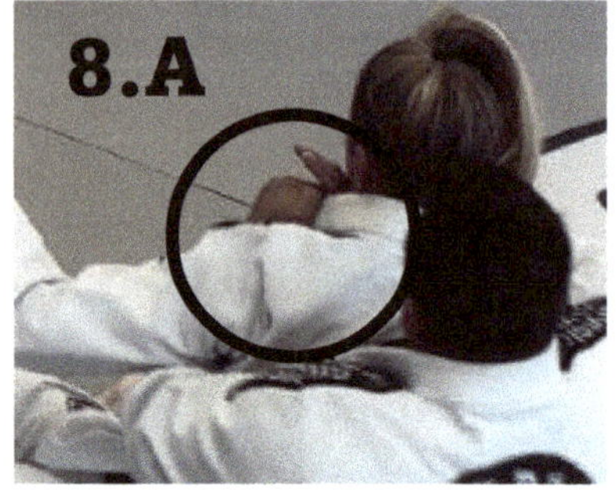

8.A - When securing your opponent', use your LEFT hand to open the collar and place your RIGHT hand deep inside across their neck and grip the collar.

7

Control the hips throughout the roll and reach over to grip your opponent's shoulder to stop from rolling away.

8

Grip the opponent's shoulder or collar and pull them into back mount and get your hooks in with both legs.

Important Details

10.A - When getting your grips, use one hand to grip the collar and the other to come under your opponent's arm and grip their wrist for more control.

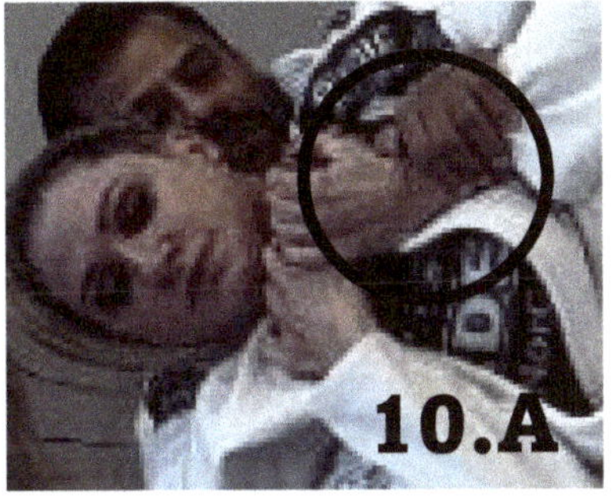

10.B - When getting hooks, your ankles should not be crossed as it could lead to a submission and failure to get points in a competition.

9

As you get your hooks in, immediately reach over and under with both hands into the seatbelt position.

10

Extend your legs and pull backward with your arms to stretch out your opponent.

1. Reach under your opponent's head with your LEFT hand and grip their LEFT shoulder.

2. Scoot your trapped foot out and push down on your opponent's thighs to create space to escape. For added control, you can grip your opponent's pants and maintain your grip throughout steps 2 to 4.

3. Continue to push down on your opponent's thigh until your foot is free and maintain control of your opponent's shoulder.

4. Once your foot is free, reach over with your foot and lock both of your opponent's legs. As your reach over with your leg, try to hook your opponent's foot and maintain throughout steps 4 to 6.

5. Sit up onto your LEFT knee and squeeze your RIGHT knee together to maintain control of your opponent. If possible, reach all the way through with your foot and hold your opponent by squeezing your **legs** together

6. As you posture up, pull up on your opponent to bring them to their side to create space. You need to create space behind your opponent in order to initiate the forward roll. As you initiate your roll, you can grip your opponent's pants or belt to control their direction during the movement

7. Perform a forward roll across your opponent towards their back while maintaining the hook on their leg to roll them.

8. Control the hips throughout the roll and reach over to grip your opponent's shoulder to stop from rolling away. As you roll, use your hands and feet to control your opponent and not allow them to create too much space.

9.   As you take the back, get your hooks in, immediately reach over and under with both hands into the seatbelt position.

10.   Extend your legs and pull backward with your arms to stretch out your opponent. When getting your grips, use one hand to grip the collar and the other to come under your opponent's arm and grip their wrist for more control. When getting hooks, your ankles should not be crossed as it could lead to a submission and failure to get points in a competition.

Application

This technique will be a little more difficult, but it can be effective in tricking your opponent.

The focus of this variation is on trapping the leg and maintaining control as you start to pass. Use the other variations to free your leg but you'll need to immediately lock their leg.

This technique can work when you're on side control and faking going to mount but instead want to roll into taking the back. In either case, you'll need to control the legs and maintain your hook.

1

Reach under your opponent's head with your LEFT hand and grip their LEFT shoulder.

2

Scoot your trapped foot out and push down on your opponent's thighs to create space to escape.

Important Details

2.A - For added control, you can grip your opponent's pants and maintain your grip throughout steps 2 to 4.

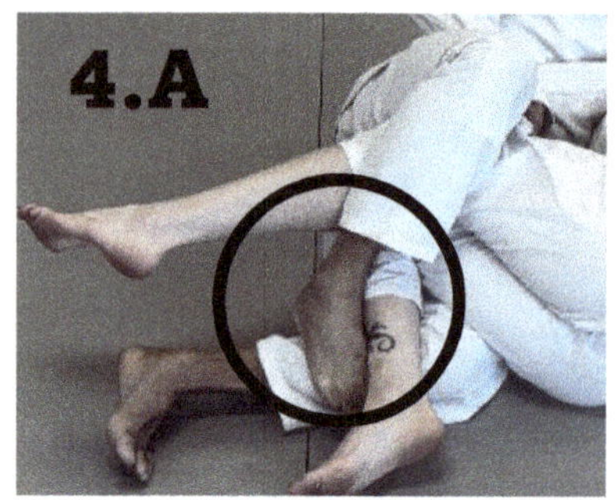

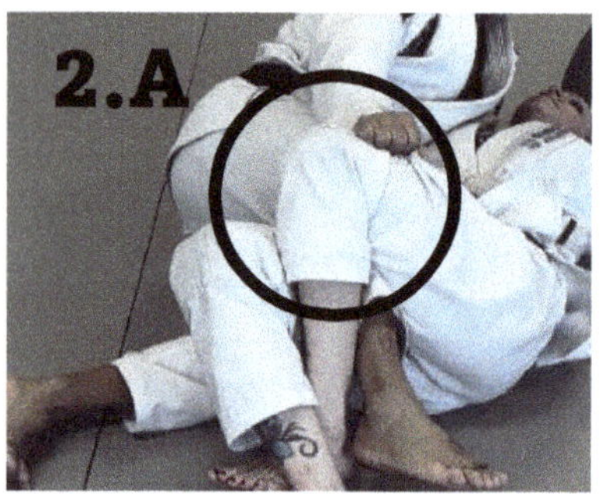

4.A - As your reach over with your leg, try to hook your opponent's foot and maintain throughout steps 4 to 6.

3

Continue to push down on their thigh until your foot is free and maintain control of your opponent's shoulder.

4

Once your foot is free, reach over with your foot and lock both of your opponent's legs.

Important Details

5.A - If possible, reach all the way through with your foot and hold your opponent by squeezing your **legs** together.

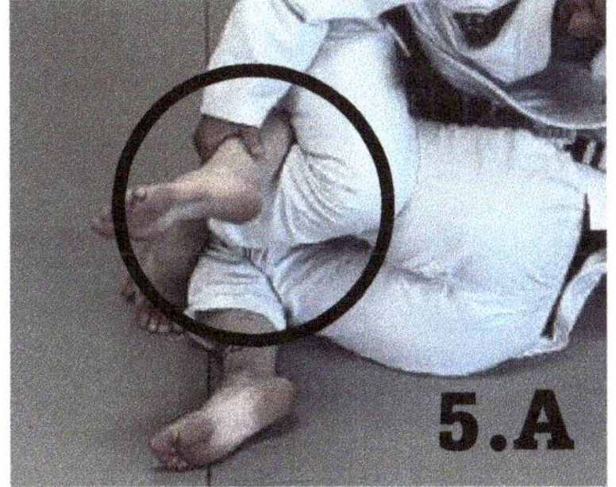

6.A - You need to create space behind your opponent in order to initiate the forward roll.

5

Sit up onto your LEFT knee and squeeze your RIGHT knee together to maintain control of your opponent.

6

As you posture up, pull up on your opponent to bring them to their side to create space.

Important Details

6.B - As you initiate your roll, you can grip your opponent's pants or belt to control their direction during the movement.

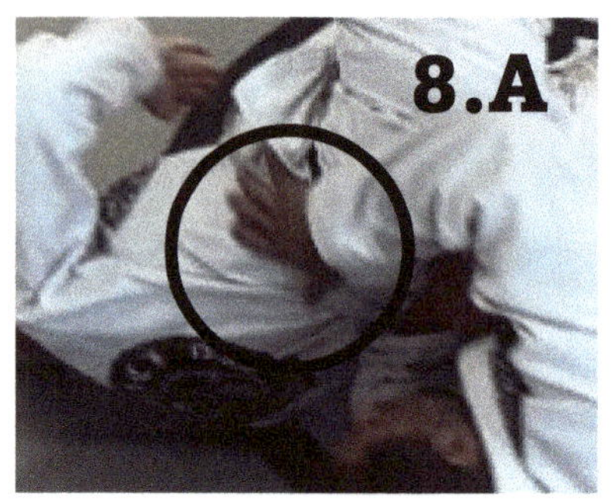

8.A - As you roll, use your hands and feet to control your opponent and not allow them to create too much space.

7

Perform a forward roll across your opponent towards their back while maintaining the hook on their leg to roll them.

8

Control the hips throughout the roll and reach over to grip your opponent's shoulder to stop from rolling away.

Important Details

10.A - When getting your grips, use one hand to grip the collar and the other to come under your opponent's arm and grip their wrist for more control.

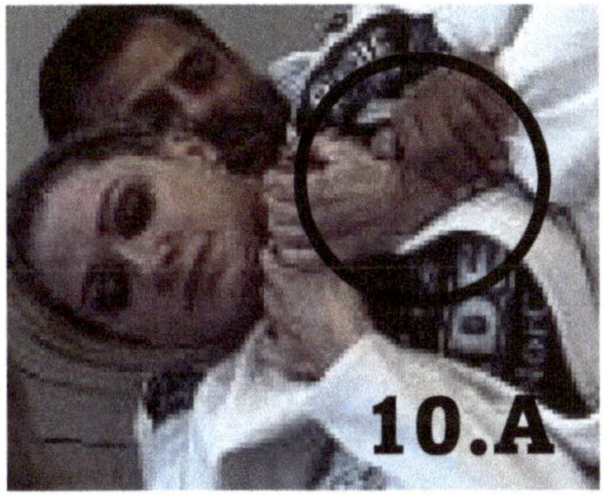

10.B - When getting hooks, your ankles should not be crossed as it could lead to a submission and failure to get points in a competition.

9

As you take the back, get your hooks in, reach over and under with both hands into the seatbelt position.

10

Extend your legs and pull backward with your arms to stretch out your opponent.

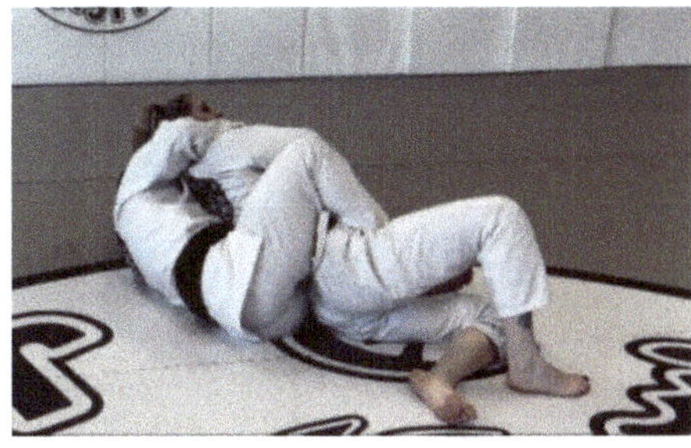

1. Reach under your opponent's head with your LEFT hand and grip their collar above their LEFT shoulder.

2. Bring your LEFT knee up against your opponent's thigh and shift your weight to that side.

3. With your LEFT hand, pull your opponent's collar up and over, using your whole body to lift them onto their LEFT side. For added control, you can grip your opponent's pants and maintain your grip throughout steps 2 to 4.

4. Once your opponent is turned over, quickly slide your knee in behind your opponent into their lower back. Your knee should be placed deep into the lower back to prevent them from laying back down.

5. Lay down behind your opponent and reach under their arm and across with your RIGHT hand and grip their collar. The grip on the collar is very important because you will need maintained control throughout steps 5 to 10.

6. Pull your opponent to the opposite side using your RIGHT hand and leaning with your whole body. Use the leg that was trapped to help pull your opponent and that foot will become the first hook when taking the back.

7. Turn to your side while continuing to pull down on your opponent's collar and hook in with your RIGHT foot. As you pull your opponent across, your foot remains against their leg as the first hook to prevent them from escaping.

8. Roll them to the side until your LEFT leg is out from under their body and bring over to place your second hook. Pull down on your opponent's collar will help move them to their side and free your foot to apply your second hook.

9. As you take the back, get your hooks in, immediately reach over and under with both hands into the seatbelt position.

10. Extend your legs and pull backward with your arms to stretch out your opponent. When getting your grips, use one hand to grip the collar and the other to come under your opponent's arm and grip their wrist for more control. When getting hooks, your ankles should not be crossed as it could lead to a submission and failure to get points in a competition.

Application

For this technique you will need to have power to pull your opponent up in order to create space.

The focus should be to create as much space as possible to allow yourself to slide in behind your opponent.

When taking the back, you will use your tapped leg as your first hook as you pull your opponent to the other side. You'll need to build upon your control by adding the second hook and gripping the collar to prevent them from rolling away.

1

Reach under your opponent's head with your LEFT hand and grip their collar above their LEFT shoulder.

2

Slide your LEFT knee up against their thigh and shift your weight to that side.

Important Details

3.A - For added control, you can grip your opponent's pants and maintain your grip throughout steps 2 to 4.

4.A - Your knee should be placed deep into the lower back to prevent them from laying back down.

3

With your LEFT hand, pull your opponent's collar up and over, using your whole body to lift them onto their LEFT side.

4

Once your opponent is turned over, quickly slide your knee in behind your opponent into their lower back.

Important Details

5.A - The grip on the collar is very important because you will need maintained control throughout steps 5 to 10.

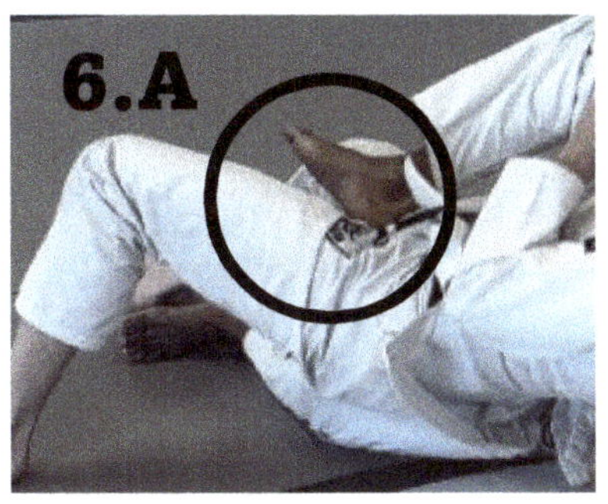

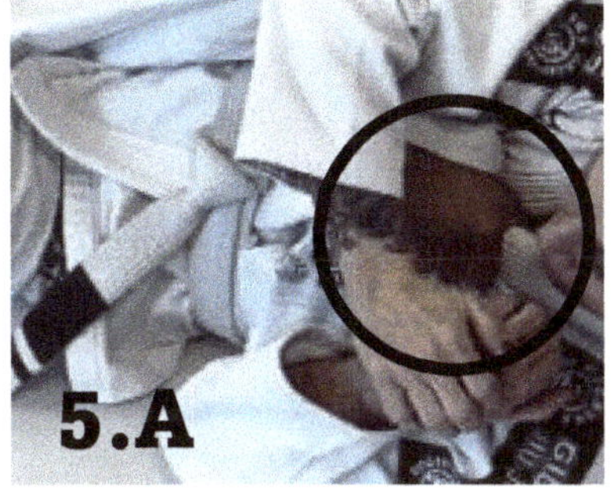

6.A - Use the leg that was trapped to help pull your opponent and that foot will become the first hook when taking the back.

5

Lay behind your opponent and reach under their arm and across with your RIGHT hand and grip their collar.

6

Pull your opponent to the opposite side using your RIGHT hand and leaning with your whole body.

Important Details

7.A - As you pull your opponent across, your foot remains against their leg as the first hook to prevent them from escaping.

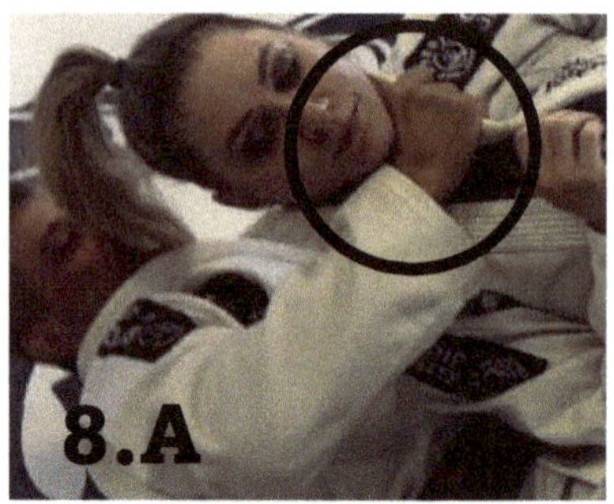

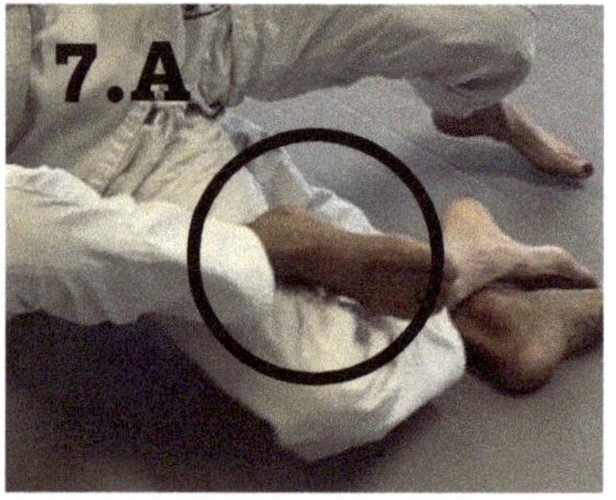

8.A - Pull down on your opponent's collar will help move them to their side and free your foot to apply your second hook.

7

Turn to your side while continuing to pull down on your opponent's collar and hook in with your RIGHT foot.

8

Roll them to the side until your LEFT leg is out from under their body and bring over to place your second hook.

Important Details

10.A - When getting your grips, use one hand to grip the collar and the other to come under your opponent's arm and grip their wrist for more control.

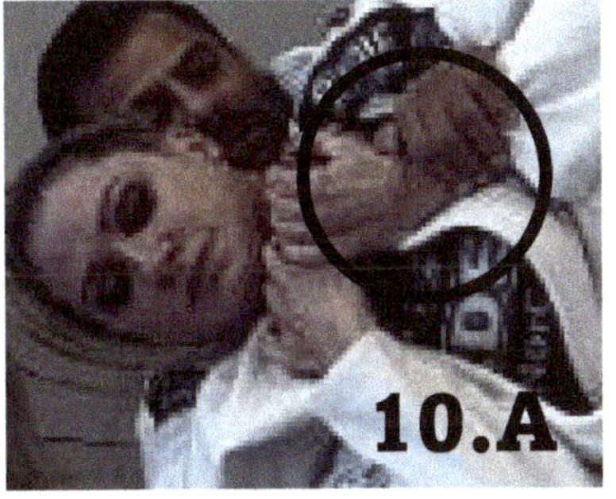

10.B - When getting hooks, your ankles should not be crossed as it could lead to a submission and failure to get points in a competition.

9

As you take the back, get your hooks in, reach over and under with both hands into the seatbelt position.

10

Extend your legs and pull backward with your arms to stretch out your opponent.

Drills for Passing Opponent's GUARD

111

Guard Pass Drill 1

Important Tips

Start with your feet shoulder width apart with your hands on your partner's knees and knees slightly bent.

Do not cross your feet anytime in this drill or Jiu-Jitsu. Use this exercise to drill good technique.

1. Start with your opponent's feet flat on the floor, place both hands on top of your partner's knees and keep your hips back.

2. Take a big step with your RIGHT foot to your RIGHT side while keeping both hands on your partner's knees.

3. Step with your LEFT foot bringing it shoulder width apart from your RIGHT foot and place your LEFT hand on top of your partner's LEFT knee.

4. Reach down and touch the mat with your RIGHT hand while keeping your hips at a neutral height and your LEFT hand on your partner's LEFT knee.

5. Take a big step with your LEFT foot to your LEFT side in front of your partner's RIGHT foot.

6. Switch your hands over so your LEFT hand and RIGHT hand are now both at the corresponding knee of your partner.

7. Take another big step with your RIGHT foot to your original starting position with your hips facing your opponent and feet shoulder width apart.

8. Continue the exercise by repeating steps 1-7 and taking the first big step to your LEFT using your LEFT foot toward your partner's RIGHT side.

Guard Pass Drill 1

Drill Description

This drill will help you build upon your abilities and gain a better understanding of the fundamental movements in Jiu-Jitsu.

There will be a variety of passes and submissions that will be available to you as well.

The difficult part of this drill will be the hand and foot coordination you will need to learn. The movement seems simple, but it can get difficult when stringing multiple reps together so keep focused on your feet placement and not jumping from side to side.

Important Tip1

Start with your feet shoulder width apart, hands on their knees and knees slightly bent.

Important Tip 2

Do not cross your feet anytime in this drill. Use this exercise to drill good technique.

Guard Pass Drill 1

Steps for this Drill

1 - Start with your partner's feet flat on the floor, place both hands on top of your partner's knees and keep your hips back.

2 - Take a big step with your RIGHT foot to your RIGHT side while keeping both hands on your partner's knees.

3 - Step with your LEFT foot bringing it shoulder width apart from your RIGHT foot and place your LEFT hand on top of your partner's LEFT knee.

4 - Reach down and touch the mat with your RIGHT hand while keeping your hips at a neutral height and your LEFT hand on your partner's LEFT knee.

Drill Description

5 - Take a big step with your LEFT foot to your LEFT side in front of your partner's RIGHT foot.

6 - Switch your hands over so your LEFT hand and RIGHT hand are now both at the corresponding knee of your partner.

7 - Take another big step with your RIGHT foot to your original starting position with your hips facing your opponent and feet shoulder width apart.

8 - Continue the exercise by repeating steps 1-7 and taking the first big step to your LEFT using your LEFT foot toward your partner's RIGHT side.

Important Details

1.A - Avoid pulling on your opponent's ankle as you want them think you are attempting to pass their guard and not going for a submission.

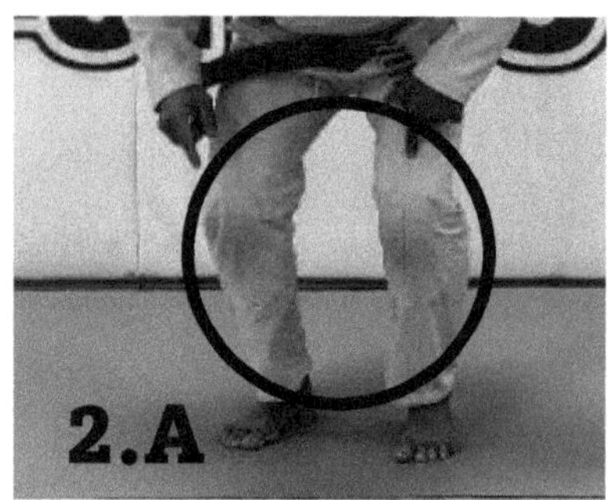

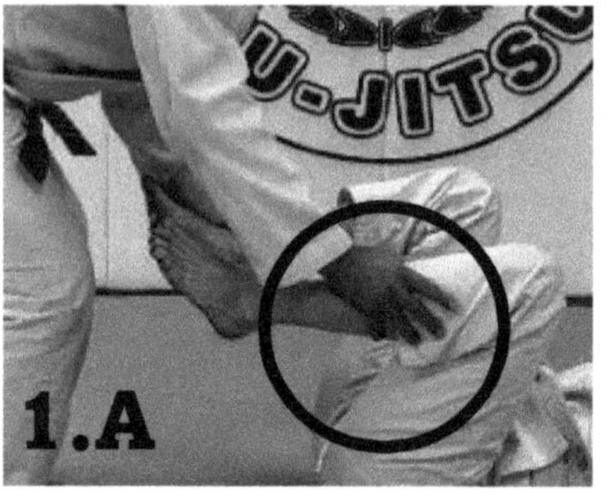

2.A - As you take your two steps to the RIGHT, keep your feet spaced apart and avoid crossing your feet.

1

Start with your hands on your opponent's knees, hips back, and push their legs forward.

2

From step 3 of the drill, take two short steps to your RIGHT bringing your feet together.

Important Details

3.A - Keep your weight down and hunched over. Do not stand straight up or lean forward to avoid becoming off balance.

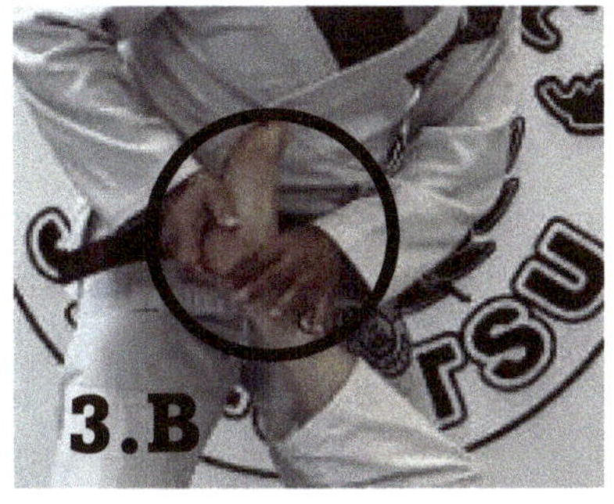

3.B - The opponent's ankle needs to be hooked at the bone and deep into your armpit to be the most effective.

3

Wrap your arm around your opponent's ankle and bring it under your armpit gripping their foot with your bicep.

4

Holding on to their ankle, sit back and wrap your legs around your opponent's leg to finish the submission.

Guard Pass Drill 2

Important Tips

Start with your feet shoulder width apart, slightly bent, with your hands on your partner's knees and feet on your hips.

You need to grip your partner's pants behind your partner's knees. When you step back, you need to pull back and down.

1. Start with your opponent's feet flat on the floor, grip your partner's pants behind the knees and keep your hips back.

2. Take a big step backward with both feet as you pull down on your partner's knees until their feet touch the mat.

3. With your LEFT foot, take a big step toward your partner's RIGHT side while continuing to grip your partner's pants.

4. Step with your RIGHT foot bringing it together with your LEFT while continuing to grip your partner's pants.

5. Bring your RIGHT knee down on top of your partner's belly, with your LEFT hand, grab their collar while maintaining your grip on their pants with your RIGHT hand.

6. Release the collar and take a step back with your RIGHT foot and bring it together with your LEFT leg. Continue to maintain your grip on the pants with your RIGHT hand.

7. Take a big step with your RIGHT leg back to its starting position in front of your partner's foot and regrip the pants with your LEFT hand.

8. Return your LEFT foot to its starting position; continue the exercise by stepping with your RIGHT foot and repeating the drill.

Drill Description

For this drill, we will build upon the first technique you practiced with proper foot movement.

This technique will focus on passing to side control knee on belly, but it can also be applied to a general pass by dropping down to side control.

You will want to focus on the movement and control of the knee of your opponent. As you pass you will want to maintain, or obtain, more points of contact for added control. This drill emphasizes control of the knees and pressure using knee on belly.

Important Tip 1

Start with your feet shoulder width apart, slightly bent, with your hands on your partner's knees and feet on your hips.

Important Tip 2

You need to grip your opponent's pants behind your partner's knees. When you step back, you need to pull back and down.

119

Steps for this Drill

1 - Start with your partner's feet on your hips, grip your partner's pants behind the knees and keep your hips back.

2 - Take a big step backward with both feet as you pull down on your partner's knees until their feet touch the mat.

3 - With your LEFT foot, take a big step toward your partner's RIGHT side while continuing to grip your partner's pants.

4 - Step with your RIGHT foot bringing it together with your LEFT while continuing to grip your partner's pants.

Steps for this Drill

5 - Bring your RIGHT knee down on top of your partner's belly, with your LEFT hand, grab their collar while maintaining your grip on their pants with your RIGHT hand.

6 - Release the collar and take a step back with your RIGHT foot and bring it together with your LEFT leg. Continue to maintain your grip on the pants with your RIGHT hand.

7 - Take a big step with your RIGHT leg back to its starting position in front of your partner's foot and regrip the pants with your LEFT hand.

8 - Return your LEFT foot to its starting position; continue the exercise by stepping with your RIGHT foot and repeating the drill to the other side.

Guard Pass Drill 3

Important Tips

Grip your partner's pants and insert your thumb into the cuffs.
Curl the pants with your thumb until your fingers are covered.

You cannot grip the pants with your fingers inside. Your thumb
can be used to curl the pants but cannot stay inside.

1. Start with your partner's feet on your hips, grip your partner's
    pants behind the knees and keep your hips back.

2. Switch your grip with your RIGHT hand by grabbing onto your
    partner's RIGHT leg so there are two hands on one leg.

3. Take a big step back with your RIGHT leg while maintaining
    control of your partner's RIGHT leg.

4. Pull back on your partner's leg using both of your hands
    gripping their pants.

5. Release the pants with your LEFT hand and take a step in
    towards your opponent while maintaining your grip on the
    pants with your RIGHT hand.

6. Place your RIGHT knee down for knee on belly as you post
    your LEFT foot out for stability and grip their collar with your
    LEFT hand.

7. Come off your knee and take a big step with your LEFT leg
    back to its starting position in front of your partner's foot.

8. Return your RIGHT foot to its starting position; continue the
    exercise by stepping with your RIGHT foot and repeating the
    drill to the other side.

Drill Description

Similar to the previous technique, the idea for this drill is to maintain control of your opponent and creating open space for you to enter.

In this drill, you'll need to obtain a solid

grip on the pants as shown below in the important tips. Practice your grip as well as it will benefit you in more techniques.

Again, as in the last drill you will want to establish points of control which will include the pant cuff, knee on belly, and the added grip on the collar.

Important Tip 1

Grip your partner's pants and insert your thumb into the cuffs. Curl the pants until your fingers are covered.

Important Tip 2

You cannot grip the pants with your fingers inside. Your thumb can be used to curl the pants but cannot stay inside.

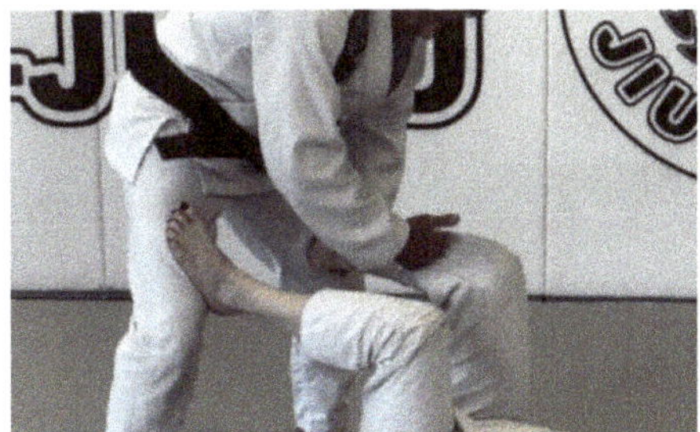

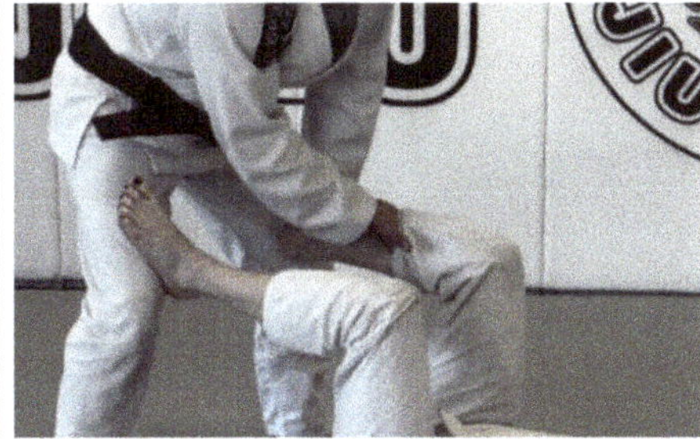

Steps for this Drill

1 - Start with your partner's feet on your hips, grip your partner's pants behind the knees and keep your hips back.

2 - Switch your grip with your RIGHT hand by grabbing onto your partner's RIGHT leg so there are two hands on one leg.

3 - Take a big step back with your RIGHT leg while maintaining control of your partner's RIGHT leg.

4 - Pull back on your partner's leg using both of your hands gripping their pants.

Guard Pass Drill 3

Steps for this Drill

5 - Release the pants with your LEFT hand and take a step in towards your opponent while maintaining your grip on the pants with your RIGHT hand.

6 - Place your RIGHT knee down for knee on belly as you post your LEFT foot out for stability and grip their collar with your LEFT hand.

7 - Come off your knee and take a big step with your LEFT leg back to its starting position in front of your partner's foot.

8 - Return your RIGHT foot to its starting position; continue the exercise by stepping with your RIGHT foot and repeating the drill to the other side.

Guard Pass Drill 4

Important Tips

As you go through the steps, keep your posture up, your hips down, and your head in a neutral position.

Do not bend over when trying to pass as you'll lose balance and put yourself at risk of getting swept by your opponent.

1. Start with your partner's feet on your hips, grip your partner's pants behind the knees and keep your hips back.

2. Bring your RIGHT elbow down on the inside of your partner's LEFT shin and push the leg off your hip.

3. Take a step with your RIGHT leg in tight against the inside of your partner's LEFT thigh.

4. With your LEFT hand, drive your partner's RIGHT leg down as you lift your LEFT leg up and over.

5. As you take your step, control the leg with your LEFT hand and grip your partner's collar with your RIGHT hand.

6. Turn your hips and bring your RIGHT knee down so it is touching the mat in line with your partner's belt/hips.

7. Come off your knee and posture up into your standing position from step 5 while maintaining control of the collar.

8. Step back in-between your opponent's guard and regrip the pants; continue by repeating the drill to the other side.

Guard Pass Drills

Drill Description

We are progressively increasing the complexity of the movements with this drill continuing to build upon the control elements of your opponent.

In this drill you'll focus on your grips and control of your opponent's legs.

Additionally, this drill will help you build awareness of your posture and ability to pass the guard. A good base, or posture, will help ensure you do not get swept or present the opportunity to your opponent to grip your collar to break your posture.

Important Tip 1

As you go through the steps, keep your posture up, your hips down, and your head in a neutral position.

Important Tip 2

Do no bend over when trying to pass as you'll lose balance and put yourself at risk of getting swept by your opponent.

Guard Pass Drill 4

Steps for this Drill

1 - Start with your partner's feet on your hips, grip your partner's pants behind the knees and keep your hips back.

2 - Bring your RIGHT elbow down on the inside of your partner's LEFT shin and push the leg off your hip.

3 - Take a step with your RIGHT leg in tight against the inside of your partner's LEFT thigh.

4 - With your LEFT hand, drive your partner's RIGHT leg down as you lift your LEFT leg up and over.

Guard Pass Drill 4

Steps for this Drill

5 - As you take your step, control the leg with your LEFT hand and grip your partner's collar with your RIGHT hand.

6 - Turn your hips and bring your RIGHT knee down so it is touching the mat in line with your partner's belt/hips.

7 - Come off your knee and posture up into your standing position from step 5 while maintaining control of the collar.

8 - Step back in-between your opponent's guard and regrip the pants; continue by repeating the drill to the other side.

Important Details

1.A - When starting to pass, grip their pants and use it to control your opponent's knee and prevent them from regaining guard.

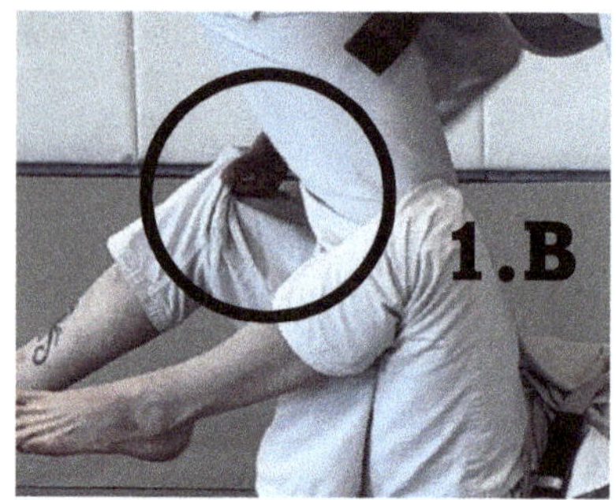

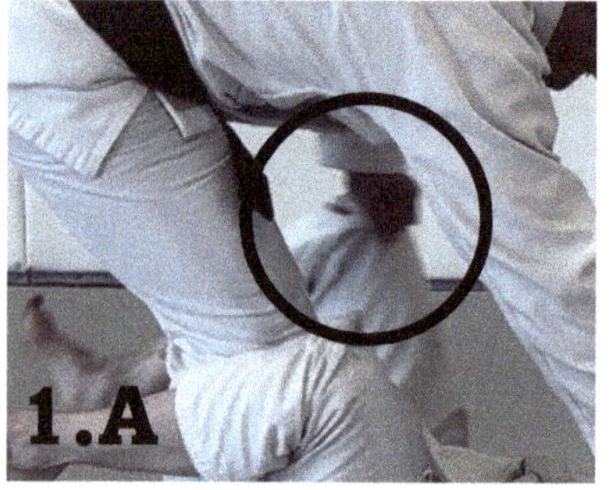

1.B - After pushing the knee down and stepping over your opponent's leg, maintain control of their leg until your knee comes down to the mat.

1

Starting from <u>step 5</u>, with your RIGHT hand grip their collar, push their knee down and step over with your LEFT leg.

2

Turn your hips and bring your RIGHT knee down so it is touching the mat in line with your partner's belt/hips.

Important Details

2.A - Throughout the steps, use the collar to control your opponent and prevent them from scooting back or creating space by hip escaping.

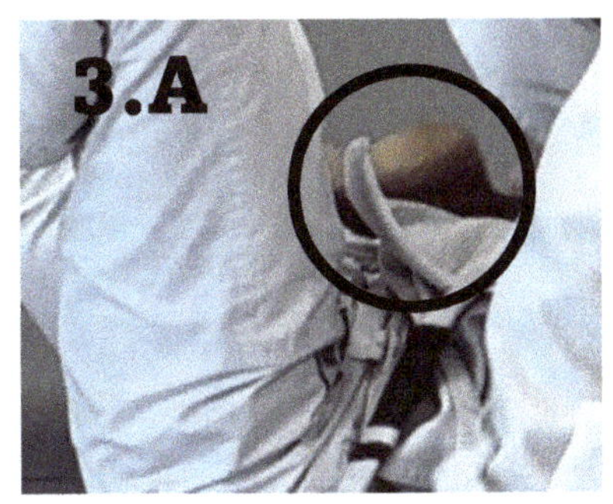

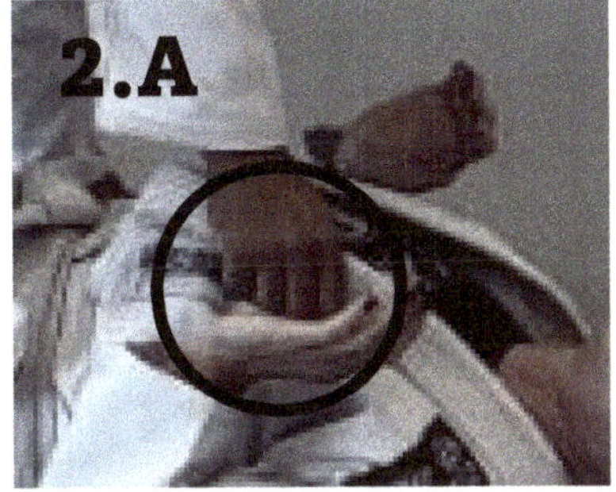

3.A - As your knee comes down, your foot will stay on the hips as you sit back into side control.

3

With your knee touching the mat, release the collar, sit back and hug your opponent under their LEFT arm.

4

Pull your RIGHT leg out from under you, slide it up near their shoulder and gain hon kesa gatame side control.

Guard Pass Drill 5

Important Tips

Keep your hands on your partner's knees and switch them at the ending position to LEFT hand to LEFT knee, etc..

 At the ending position, look back at your opponent through the gap in your arm.

1. Start with your partner's feet on your hips, grip your partner's pants behind the knees and keep your hips back.

2. Take a big step backward with both feet as you pull down on your partner's knees until their feet touch the mat.

3. You need to start with your hips back and arms extended so you have space to move.

4. With your LEFT leg, step in between your partner's legs and turn your hips to your RIGHT with feet pointed forward towards their LEFT foot.

5. Swing your RIGHT foot around behind you until your feet are parallel and facing away from your partner. Continue to look back at your partner.

6. Take a step forward with your RIGHT foot and return your LEFT foot to its starting position facing your partner.

7. With your RIGHT leg, step in between your partner's legs and turn your hips to your LEFT with feet pointed forward towards their RIGHT foot.

8. Swing your LEFT foot around behind you until your feet are parallel and facing away from your partner and then return to the starting position to repeat the drill.

Guard Pass Drill 5

Drill Description

For this drill, the focus will be on your movement and hand placement when passing the guard.

This is another drill where you'll learn to hide your intent and fake going one direction and going towards another.

The value in learning this technique will be when opponents have good open guard and are trying to hook your legs as you try to pass. You will need to grow your abilities and be comfortable navigating their hooks while keeping control of your opponent.

Important Tip 1

Keep your hands on your partner's knees and switch them at the ending position to LEFT hand to LEFT knee, etc..

Important Tip 2

At the ending position, look back at your opponent through the gap in your arm.

Steps for this Drill

1 - Start with your partner's feet on your hips, grip your partner's pants behind the knees and keep your hips back.

2 - Take a big step backward with both feet as you pull down on your partner's knees until their feet touch the mat.

3 - You need to start with your hips back and arms extended so you have space to move.

4 - With your LEFT leg, step in between your partner's legs and turn your hips to your RIGHT with feet pointed forward towards their LEFT foot.

Guard Pass Drill 5

Steps for this Drill

5 - Swing your RIGHT foot around behind you until your feet are parallel and facing away from your partner. Continue to look back at your partner.

6 - Take a step forward with your RIGHT foot and return your LEFT foot to its starting position facing your partner.

7 - With your RIGHT leg, step in between your partner's legs and turn your hips to your LEFT with feet pointed forward towards their RIGHT foot.

8 - Swing your LEFT foot around behind you until your feet are parallel and facing away from your partner and then return to the starting position to repeat the drill.

Important Details

1.A - When initiating the technique, face your opponent and make them think you are going forward to pass.

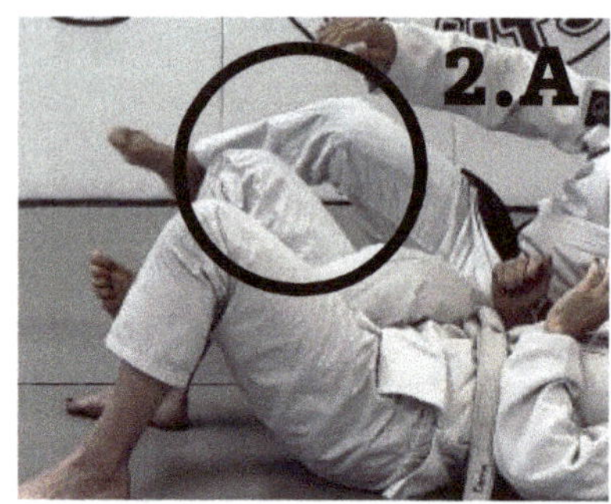

2.A - When sitting down, extend your RIGHT leg away from your opponent to create stability as you attempt to pass.

1

Starting from <u>step 5</u>, have your RIGHT hand grip your opponent's RIGHT pant leg.

2

Sit backward towards your opponent's RIGHT side and grip their collar with your LEFT hand.

Important Details

2.B - As you sit down grip the pants and maintain control of your partner's leg until you are ready to pass.

3.A - As you pass, apply pressure against your opponent's leg and turn your knee as you scoot back to free your leg.

3

Reach around and grip the shoulder, push down on your opponent's leg, scoot your hips back, and pull your leg free.

4

Pass the legs and come down onto your opponent into 100 kilos with your LEFT arm under your opponent's head.

Guard Pass Drill 6

Important Tips

Your head will start in the middle to begin the drill and then be on the same side as your legs to initiate the technique.

Use your hands to support your head and your shoulder down on your partner's hips. Avoid putting too much pressure on your neck.

1. Start with your knees on the ground in between your partner's legs with your hands down on either side.

2. Staying on all fours, place your head down onto the mat to your partner's LEFT side.

3. Raise your knees off the ground and lift your LEFT leg straight up into the air.

4. Using upward momentum, kick your leg up and swing your body to your LEFT side.

5. When you land, come down onto your LEFT leg SOFTLY followed by your RIGHT leg.

6. Pick your head up and place it to the opposite side of your partner with your hands still planted on either side.

7. Place your head down onto the mat, with your hands supporting you, and lift your butt into the air.

8. Lift your RIGHT leg into the air and use the upward momentum to jump to the other side to continue the drill.

Drill Description

Here is another drill that will help grow your technique and abilities in Jiu-Jitsu.

This is another drill that seems simple but will pay huge dividends if executed correctly. The focus

will be on getting your leg up high to clear your opponent's legs.

This is my favorite drill to train because it can help you in multiple situations. For example, when in side control and your opponent over commits to their hip escape, this movement will help you jump to the other side and reestablish control.

Important Tip 1

Your head will start in the middle to begin the drill and be on the same side as your legs to initiate the technique.

Important Tip 2

Use your hands to support your head and your shoulder down on your partner's hips. Avoid putting too much pressure on your neck.

Guard Pass Drill 6

Steps for this Drill

1 - Start with your knees on the ground in between your partner's legs with your hands down on either side.

2 - Staying on all fours, place your head down onto the mat to your partner's LEFT side.

3 - Raise your knees off the ground and lift your LEFT leg straight up into the air.

4 - Using upward momentum, kick your leg up and swing your body to your LEFT side.

Guard Pass Drill 6

Steps for this Drill

5 - When you land, come down onto your LEFT leg SOFTLY followed by your RIGHT leg.

6 - Pick your head up and place it to the opposite side of your partner with your hands still planted on either side.

7 - Place your head down onto the mat, with your hands supporting you, and lift your butt into the air.

8 - Lift your RIGHT leg into the air and use the upward momentum to jump to the other side to continue the drill.

Important Details

1.A - Use your elbows to squeeze your opponent to control their hips when setting up the pass.

2.A - You can reach over to the opposite side and grip or block your opponent's leg to prevent them from raising or opening their leg to block your pass.

1

Starting from <u>step 2 of the drill</u>, grip your opponent's belt and bring your knees in towards your opponent's butt.

2

Raise your knees off the ground, apply downward pressure onto your opponent, lift your RIGHT leg straight up into the air.

Important Details

3.A - When jumping to the opposite side, come down onto your toes, landing with one foot at a time.

3.B - When landing on the opposite side, use your hand for stability and accessible to grip your opponent.

3

Using upward momentum, kick your RIGHT leg up and swing your body to your opponent's LEFT side, one foot at a time.

4

As both feet come down, slide your RIGHT knee towards your opponent as you grip under their neck into 100 kilo side control.

Guard Pass Drill 7

Important Tips

Get into a flow where your partner drops and lifts their legs in sequence repeat the drill faster to build your reflexes.

As you pass to each side, you can practice switching from hand on the leg of your partner or on the mat as you step across.

1. Start on your partner's RIGHT side, their LEFT leg in the air, your head and LEFT hand hugging their leg, and your RIGHT hand planted on the floor.

2. Lean forward against your partner's leg as you slice your LEFT leg across your partner's leg until your knee and foot touch the mat.

3. Step over with your RIGHT leg and post your foot while continuing to hug your partner's LEFT leg.

4. Rotate your body towards your partner by bringing your RIGHT leg in towards their LEFT hip.

5. Your partner will switch their legs by lowering their LEFT leg and lifting their RIGHT leg up into the air.

6. Place your head under your partner's RIGHT leg while hugging with your RIGHT hand and come off your LEFT knee.

7. Lean forward against your partner's leg as you slice your RIGHT leg across your partner's leg until your knee and foot touch the mat.

8. Rotate your body towards your partner and continue by having your partner lift their opposite leg to repeating the drill.

Drill Description

This drill will help you learn to navigate your opponent's open guard and can be used to navigate several passing techniques.

For this drill, you will want to focus on pressure on the leg of

your opponent that you're using to pass and control of the leg down on the mat to prevent the close guard or sweep.

In practice, this technique can be used to stack your opponent by applying forward pressure on the leg that's up and sliding your body through to the other side to achieve side control.

Important Tip 1

Get into a flow where your partner drops and lifts their legs in sequence repeat the drill faster to build your reflexes.

Important Tip 2

As you pass to each side, you can practice switching from hand on the leg of your partner or on the mat as you step across.

Steps for this Drill

1 - Start on your partner's RIGHT side, their LEFT leg in the air, your head and LEFT hand hugging their leg, and your RIGHT hand planted on the floor.

2 - Lean forward against your partner's leg as your slice your LEFT leg across your partner's leg until you knee and foot touch the mat.

3 - Step over with your RIGHT leg and post your foot while continuing to hug your partner's LEFT leg.

4 - Rotate your body towards your partner by bringing your RIGHT leg in towards their LEFT hip.

Steps for this Drill

5 - Your partner will switch their legs by lowering their LEFT leg and lifting their RIGHT leg up into the air.

6 - Place your head under your partner's RIGHT leg while hugging with your RIGHT hand and come off your LEFT knee.

7 - Lean forward against your partner's leg as you slice your RIGHT leg across your partner's leg until your knee and foot touch the mat.

8 - Rotate your body towards your partner and continue by having your partner lift their opposite leg to repeating the drill.

Guard Pass Drill 8

Important Tips

As you initiate the drill, your elbows should pass your partner's legs as if you're reaching down to touch the mat.

When you're finish the drill, clasp your hands together and pull your partner's hips into your thighs for maximum control.

1. Start with your partner's feet on your hips, grip your partner's pants behind the knees and keep your hips back.

2. Release the pants and bring your hands straight down to the mat in between your partner's legs while they keep their legs on your hips.

3. With both hands, reach around your partner's legs so that their legs are sitting on top of your biceps/shoulders.

4. Once you reach around, come down to your knees and you lean forward onto your partner making them carry some of your weight.

5. Using the space created by leaning forward (step 6), slide both knees under your partner's hips so that their butt is elevated off the mat onto your thighs.

6. Throughout the drill, you can grip your partner's belt OR clasp both hands together at the belt line (good for NoGi).

7. Release your hands and slide your knees back so your opponent's butt is sitting back onto the mat.

8. Get back up to your knees and repeat the exercise at varying levels of speed.

Drill Description

This drill will aim at improve your skill in entering your opponent's guard to pass.

The early drills focused on control from the outside to pass the guard. This drill focuses on getting inside your opponent's legs and taking away their ability to control you from their open guard.

The "stack and pass" is a powerful technique as it applies a lot of pressure to your opponent while enabling you to control their base with the scoop of the legs and controlling their hips.

Important Tip 1

To initiate the drill, your elbows will pass your partner's legs as if you're reaching down to touch the mat.

Important Tip 2

When you're finish the drill, clasp your hands together and pull your partner's hips into your thighs for max control.

Steps for this Drill

1 - Start with your partner's feet on your hips, grip your partner's pants behind the knees and keep your hips back.

2 - Release the pants and bring your hands straight down to the mat in between your partner's legs while they keep their legs on your hips.

3 - With both hands, reach around your partner's legs so that their legs are sitting on top of your biceps/shoulders.

4 - Once you reach around, come down to your knees and you lean forward onto your partner making them carry some of your weight.

Steps for this Drill

5 - Using the space created by leaning forward (step 6), slide both knees under your partner's hips so that their butt is elevated off the mat onto your thighs.

6 - Throughout the drill, you can grip your partner's belt OR clasp both hands together at the belt line (good for NoGi).

7 - Release your hands and slide your knees back so your opponent's butt is sitting back onto the mat.

8 - Get back up to your knees and repeat the exercise at varying levels of speed.

Important Details

1.A - In steps 2-3, you need to create space by applying forward pressure and tucking your knees under your opponent for maximum control.

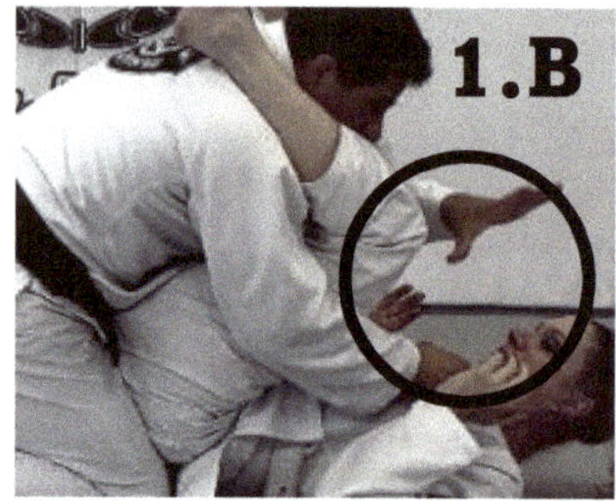

1.B - From steps 1 to 3, you will reach into your opponent's collar with your thumb inside and maintain your grip throughout the movement.

1

Start from step 5 of the drill, with your RIGHT hand open the collar, slide in your LEFT hand in and grip their collar.

2

Come off your knees and lean forward onto your opponent making them carry your weight bringing their butt off the mat.

Important Details

2.A - When leaning forward on your opponent, bring your hips forward to prevent your opponent pushing back with their legs.

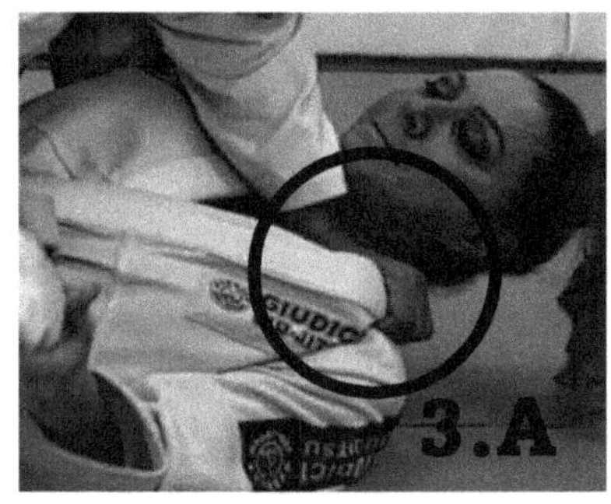

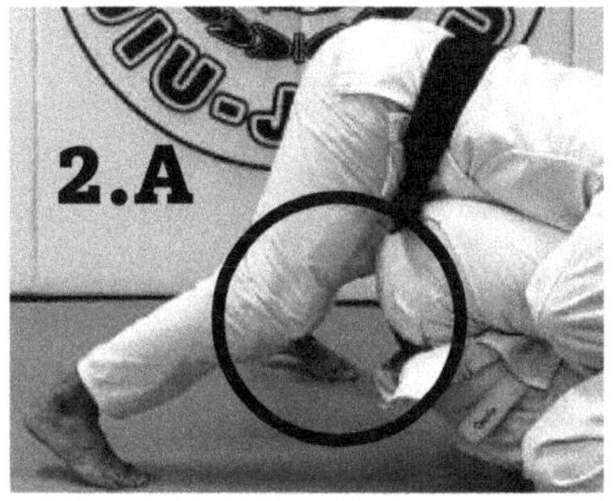

3.A - As you pass, maintain your grip on the collar and turn your elbow down to apply pressure against your opponent's throat.

3

Maintain your grip on the collar, turn inward towards your opponent and push their legs away using your shoulder.

4

Pass the legs and come down onto your opponent into 100 kilos with your LEFT arm under your opponent's head.

Appendices

Andrew 'A.J.' Morales

It has been a lifelong dream of mine to author and publish a book of my own. As an avid reader, I love learning about an author's writing process, their commitment and drive in crafting a book. I have always respected the art of writing and hope to one day author a book about leadership and organizational development which is one of my passions to teach.

In September 2022, Marcelo asked my thoughts about a book idea he had to document a series of techniques he has learned, and crafted, over the years. I thought it was a great idea because he always brings a unique perspective based on his years of traveling the world and training with some amazing BJJ practitioners. He asked if I had any experience in writing and we talked about my ideas of how to craft a book that would deliver not only the value of his experience but make it accessible to an evolving generation of readers throughout the world.

In my career I have authored several company standards, procedures, job aids, desktop instructions, and other internal communications. My degree in project management has helped me throughout my career in planning and executing major initiatives down to smaller activities like planning a road trip. I felt the combination of these skills would bring my own unique perspective to the book writing process and overall instructional details when paired with Marcelo's technical knowledge and direction.

In October 2022, I experienced a small fracture in my foot

which sidelined me and prevented me from training. I continued to attend class so I wouldn't miss important lessons, and this is when I took the opportunity to begin filming some of the techniques. I went home and began studying the instructions provided by Marcelo while taking note of the important details he would highlight when demonstrating each technique.

After having enough "footage" I developed a mockup for Marcelo to show my book ideas. In November, we began the writing process and have been collaborating ever since to bring you our first book. I couldn't be prouder and more honored to be part of this journey with Marcelo.

I hope you enjoy the book as it took many early mornings, late nights, long weekends, and lots of caffeine to achieve. Paired with the videos, I believe this book can become a staple in anyone's Jiu-Jitsu journey.

Lastly, I spent a lot of time placing "easter eggs" throughout the book via the QR codes. If you've made it this far without scanning the QR codes with your phone, I highly encourage you check them out as I tried to bring a little interactivity to the book reading experience.

From left to right: Landon Morris, Ronnie Harris, Andrew Morales, Kyle Mulhern, Memo and Abby Sainz

Acknowledgements

We would like to thank Memo and Abby for believing in Marcelo and his work enough to invest time and money into starting the first North American Giudici Jiu-Jitsu gym. Your time and dedication to the gym has helped shape our small gym into a large family of extraordinary people from students to parents. Without you our Jiu-Jitsu family would never have known what it was like to be in each other's lives, and some would never have stepped foot on the mat. Thank you.

I'd like to thank my family for supporting me while I buckled down and began writing this book. It took some early mornings and late evenings to write and edit the book and to record and edit the accompanying videos. This took time away on weekends and sometimes meant taking my laptop with me on vacations. But throughout the writing process my family encouraged me to finish and reminded me that it takes commitment to achieve the things we want in life. Thank you.

We'd like to thank Joe Moreira for taking the time to provide his thoughts and insights into the book and for his forward about Marcelo. It was an honor and a privilege to have met and trained with a bona fide Jiu-Jitsu Master. Thank you

We'd also like to thank Kyle Mulhern for giving this book a once over to provide editing and feedback. Thank you.

Lastly, we'd like to thank the readers for believing in this book enough to invest in us with your purchase. We hope to continue writing and bringing Marcelo's unique experiences to those who cannot train with him in person. Thank you.

Title Sanda:

- Chinese Boxing: – 72 fights (Striker) 58 victories -8 draws-5 losses
- 2x champion Asia (Hong Kong)
- 2x champion World (Beijing-Taiwan)
- Champion Pro National Tournament Beijing

Coach: The only foreign fighter to be hired by the Chinese government to represent China in national and international tournaments 1992/1994.

The only coach to be hired by the Chinese team to prepare their fighters in national and international competitions 2016/2017

Jiu-Jitsu:

- 5x Champion state (São Paulo)
- Champion Brazilian (Rio de Janeiro)
- 3 placed Pan American (New Beach)
- 3 placed World (Rio de Janeiro)
- Champion in International submission Fighting (São Paulo Brazil)

M.M.A (Mixed Martial Arts):

- 16 fights – 12 win – 3 loss 1 draw
- In event 11-8-win 2 loss 1 draw

Tournaments:

- Brazilian Circuit of Champions-style Free (Ibirapuera)
- Winner of the circuit-free Brazilian Style (Gina. Portuguese)

www.ingramcontent.com/pod-product-compliance
Lightning Source LLC
Chambersburg PA
CBHW061130160726
48006CB00036B/1600